Experiential Authority.

By Michael Towers MA

Published by Michael Towers
Copyrighted Material

To Dr. Samuel Berg,
Who invited me to have a conversation

Acknowledgements

To my wife and partner of these last twenty years whose knowledge, understanding, and experience of me helped challenge and shape many aspects of this book.

To my children, whose encouragement and inspiration helped me find perspective and space in which to explore my story of loss woven into my story of life.

To those who have traveled in an out of my life at various times and various chapters. I have been shaped because of those interactions and those stories. I am who I am today because of you and for that I am thankful.

Contents

Introduction

I remember sitting at the kitchen table in my parent's trailer as a little boy. The trailer sported a 1970's motif adorning the walls, yellow appliances filling up the kitchen, and different variations of plaid contrasted only by the thick shag carpet, red or green I believe. I sat there only momentarily, before launching into an adlib cut scene of a typical conversation that my parents might have. I would rattle off some typical lines, mimicking my mother and then, sliding my bottom across the cheap vinyl bench that we had for seats I would position myself in order to mimic my father before reciting his lines. If I recall correctly, my parents caught me putting on this show for myself once or twice, and I am sure like any typical parents, they found only the first time funny.

It is fair to say that I have been an observer of human interaction from a young age, fascinated with each other's relationship to one another, and the dynamics that accompany those relationships. Perhaps this fascination came out of my contentment not to get overly involved in activities but instead to sit quietly on the sidelines. From there I could take everything in, studying people. I would observe the actions and reactions of people, quietly filing that information away, as a hobbyist fills their garage or attic with found trinkets.

The outcome of these early years of

observing people was that I discovered that there was always a Speaker and there was a Listener. As these various relational dynamics played out, the role of Speaker and Listener became more defined for me. I became used to the rhythm and the interactions that each would play out with each other. I studied the various methods that the Speaker would use in which to engage the Listener. Conversely, I also studied the various methods that the Listener would engage the Speaker.

However, I also began to notice that although the Speaker always seemed to speak, the Listener did not always seem to listen. In order to entice the Listener to listen the Speaker would change their tactics. This back and forth dynamic between the Speaker and the Listener continued to captivate my curiosity as an adolescent. I would observe the various methods that the Speaker would use in order to keep the Listener's attention, always observing what the Listener would do in response. Ironically, as I became a young adult and now finding myself in a position of authority, I found that my own desire to listen was being outweighed by my desire to speak. I felt that given my newly acquired place of authority that I had something to say and my expectation was that there should be people around who would listen.

This, however, did not go as I had thought. The more authority, experience, and knowledge that I accumulated the more I wanted to speak. Yet, I was having a harder and harder time finding people who wanted to listen. In fact, it would seem that there were becoming less and less listeners and more and more speakers. If there are more speakers than there are listeners, who is listening to the speakers? Having been one of those speakers I reflected on my own question and this was my conclusion. It did not concern me who was listening to me because what was more important was that I had something to say. In light of this revelation, I was beginning to understand what was happening here. Perhaps I was not alone in this personal 'conviction' of sorts. Perhaps many people felt like they had something to say as well.

Informally, I have been fascinated with relational dynamics for quite some time, which was a motivating factor for me to return to school to get my Masters in Marriage and Family Counseling. What my educational journey provided for me was language for my unlanguaged experiences around relational dynamics. What also emerged was a deeper curiosity into the particular relational dynamics that exists between the Speaker and the Listener. It had seemed that these two dominate characters kept reappearing in my research and I began to think of them in these ways.

The Speaker seemed like the antagonist, emerging as a character that we all love to hate. My concern here, was that I continued to see entirely too much of myself in that character. The Listener on the other hand was the story's protagonist, yet there were times that I found myself describing this character with such sad and lost words, not the noble hero type descriptions I had been hoping for. The Listener's stories of pain and loss dominated my research and far too often, I found myself relating to this character just as much as I was to the Speaker.

This book then, is the presentation of a new language for these unlanguaged emotional experiences. Experiential Authority is presented, unpacked, and quantified through antidotal observations I have made out of my research and my life. I have written this book, unpacking the various related concepts of Experiential Authority using our two main characters; the Speaker and the Listener to help the reader understand the concepts. You, my reader, can decide for yourself who you most connect to, if not both of them. Through this journey of language discovery, I trust that you may find the language of Experiential Authority just as helpful for you as I did for myself.

Chapter 1 Presuppositions

Every conversation the Speaker has or the Listener has reflects their experiences, their knowledge, their understanding, and their presuppositions. They both communicate in conversation out of their acquired verbal knowledge; using language that they feel best represents their experiences. However, the Speaker and the Listener's non-verbal cues share those preconceived ideas they both have, that linger behind the conversation. These preconceived ideas, or presuppositions, are those beliefs they have about most things that in turn influence how they think, and how they act. The Speaker and the Listener reveal their prejudices, racism, biases, morals, and their ethics, which all work together to reveal the person they are.

As the Speaker and the Listener enter into conversation with one another, they bring all of those preconceived ideas – those presuppositions – along with them. As the Speaker endeavours to listen to the Listener, he or she will almost immediately begin to form opinions on the content they are hearing, along with what they are seeing. These opinions come from those ideas they had long before they sat in conversation with the Listener. These ideas regarding presuppositions make listening a very difficult task for the Speaker. As it turns out, the Speaker is not really listening to the Listener at all.

It is because of the Speaker's

presuppositions that he or she cannot be completely objective. Many professionals, as an example, felt the need to obtain some level of objectivity in their work, such as law enforcement officers, doctors, other health care workers, therapists, and counselors. Traditionally, this was because their professions would view them as the expert, being in a place of knowing, while the assumption was that those around them were not. It was further assumed that because of the accumulated knowledge one had, their knowledge, by definition, made them objective. However, it is a dangerous thing whenever someone would declare himself or herself as being objective. The Speaker can strive to be better listeners, and better communicators, and they can be aware of self and their prejudices, which will help minimize their subjective notions, but the Speaker cannot truly be objective.

Objectivity is the ability to be unbiased, non-emotive, well-differentiated, neutral, experientially detached, or if you were a fan of Star Trek: The Next Generation – Data. Data was, as some of you may know, an android who struggled to be human all the while not. However, perhaps a better comparison might be Spock, who was human (sort of) but very 'logical'. Captain Kirk continued to shoot holes into Spock's logic through every episode and movie they made, revealing the intense emotional connections that were always there, lurking beneath the surface.

These shows have done a great job portraying the fruitlessness in trying to operate within this bubble called objectivity. Yet it seems society is continuing to embrace an old idea that it is still possible for the Speaker to be truly objective. Therapists, as an example, come from the school of thought that it is entirely possible for the counselor or therapist to be objective in their work with clients. This old way of thinking called their clients patients, which defined a hierarchal relationship that revealed the presupposition that the therapist was right and the patient was not.

However, over the last thirty plus years, the terminology has changed from a patient to a client. With this change of terminology has come an acknowledgement that the therapist cannot be objective and perhaps more importantly, to be objective would end up harming the client instead of helping. Now, many professionals have taken this point-of-view, in which they acknowledge the subjective nature of humanity, and by consequence, the limitations of being truly objective. As a result, therapists and other professionals began to recognize that they were in a place of power in this conversation with their clients. This awareness of their Positional Authority helped the therapists and other professionals become more aware of their use of power in a therapeutic relationship. They recognized that their subjectivity disguised as objectivity could bring much harm to their clients and in fact, it had over the decades prior.

Could it be that such positional power,

mixed with these ideas around objectivity, might exist outside of the therapy room, and is continuing to create harm in our day-to-day relationships with one another? I hypothesize that this is indeed occurring and is one element in the foundation of Experiential Authority. Positional power places upon it the demands of knowledge and with knowledge is an embedded sense of objectivity. This is perhaps why many have a desire to approach a conversation or connection with one another objectively. The idea comes out of how we look at knowledge.

Knowledge carries with it objective characteristics, and the expectation is that if one obtains knowledge, they carry with it the responsibility of remaining objective, in order to preserve the knowledge. This idea came out of a modernist way of thinking, which helped shape our society and culture for the last few hundred years. The modernist construct was set on establishing a moral code, defining the rules related to these ideas. As a result, it became important that in knowledge there is a set of absolutes defining that knowledge. These modernistic absolutes declare that something is either right or it is wrong. These sets of absolutes are based in larger meta-truths of morality, also defined by modernist ideas. Because these moral constructs dictated human behavior, and came from a place of knowledge, it became important within society to ensure that those who held the knowledge remained objective in an effort not to erode these moral constructs.

These moral constructs, based on

objective knowledge, dictated society's behaviours, thoughts, motives, and pretty much everything that makes us human. The have permeated every aspect of our lives, dictating what is and what should be. What is interesting about these moral constructs are not the ideas of modernity itself, but instead the implication of what objective knowledge, defined by modernity, now demands from society. The implication of this objective knowledge construct is that society has created a group of individuals who understand and possess this knowledge. Their purpose, as defined by modernistic thought, is to teach the rest of society what is right and what is wrong. In order to preserve modernist's construct of objective knowledge within this modernistic society, these individuals are then set apart and honored, because of the knowledge that they have.

Society, therefore, was organized into social and economic classes, mixed together with vocational and gender descriptions, which helped us know who within society had the knowledge and by definition who did not. Through this process then, we have people obtaining superior class and description prior to obtaining knowledge, whether they were born into it or whether they obtained it through favour or reward. As part of society's social structure, we then have these sets of moral constructs already pieced out within society. These moral constructs are then redefined by the experiences of the minority before being imposed upon the majority. However, these moral constructs are already fractured due to the segregation of the initial social classes and those individuals charged with the burden of containing this objective knowledge.

It would seem that this hierarchical structure, set up to protect the objective knowledge, was doomed from the beginning. When we factor in the Reformation and what that did for the religious institution, coupled with the separation of science from religion, we can see in hindsight how fragile modernistic thought had become. Thus, over the last one hundred years a post-modernist viewpoint has emerged. However, in the effort to deconstruct the rights and wrongs imposed upon society by those in privileged power, post-modernists have seemed to overlook some of society's underlying currents that were pushing agendas. These prominent agendas being the desire to gain back, or take for themselves that privileged power used to impose upon the have-nots their experiential version of objective knowledge.

Today when someone becomes part of the societal or economic class where knowledge is expected, a new prevailing problem emerges. If just by their gender or vocational position they are in a place where knowledge is expected, the new prevailing problem becomes this idea of experiential knowledge, or "it happened to me therefore it is true." Today, we have woven into our society a move away from modernist thought, surrounding what is right and what is wrong, replaced by an individualistic and experiential right and wrong. By ignoring these underlying currents, society continues to model the very behaviour they were taught by their modernist forefathers. This is in spite of society now becoming post-modernists, giving space to the feminist movement, racial deconstruction leading to multiculturalism, and other modern societal correctives. Sadly, society continues to hold their post-modern, experiential knowledge in objective, modernistic constructs.

Ironically, the deconstructive methodology of post-modernism, in such areas as experiential learning, only muddies the waters, since the learning gained from such efforts were stuffed back into the old objective knowledge structures left over from modernist thought. If the post-modernists are deconstructing objective knowledge imposed upon them by modernists, but still striving to gain positional power through the hierarchical structures left over from modernist thought, what we end up with is a new form of knowledge structure called experiential knowledge.

Consequently, the post-modern corrective to modernism, being this idea of experiential knowledge, never addressed the positional power problem. This then creates the space for persons of perceived privilege to hold onto the positional power. Since they are able to hang onto to their positional power, they can now draw on their experiences within this new post-modern knowledge construct to help define their own objectivity, which then can be imposed upon others. The post-modernists did this instead of understanding that their very experiences, influenced by their positional power, were influencing the conversations they were having with one another. Their knowledge was experiential and collaborative, shared across socio-economic classes, but in the end, they ignored this helpful deconstruction. Instead, the ugly truth is that although they said they did not want to be 'like them'; they were in fact, striving to be 'them'.

Harm, therefore, now has no borders within society, since all of society can operate out of experiential knowledge. The Speaker does this by believing they are being objective when imposing right and wrong upon others. All the while the Speaker is oblivious to the fact that they are instead using positional authority and power to push their own subjective agenda, instead of the objective knowledge construct they thought they were still using. In the end, the corrective to this 'corrective' is admitting to one another that the Speaker cannot be objective in a relational sense; nor should they even try. The Speaker's subjectivity renders their ability to be truly objective nil. The Speaker needs to acknowledge that their knowledge is based on acquired facts and truths but is woven together with their experiences, which by definition are biased and therefore subjective.

Consequently, because this experiential knowledge is a reflection of the Speaker's prejudices, racism, biases, morals, and ethics, these presuppositions must inform the Speaker in a different methodology to employ in conversations. The Speaker's awareness of these presuppositions is an important first step in enhancing their conversations with the Listener. This new methodology is to acknowledge a 'not-knowing' with the Listener, along with a self-awareness of how the Speaker might be impacted by the Listener's own experiences. Within this conversation, truth is not deconstructed, which would erode knowledge to a place of passivity. Instead, this not-knowing stance enhances connection through a healthy balance of power, a power without position or imposed authority. Perhaps Spock may find such a thing 'illogical', but it is necessary if society is ever going to offer a healthy corrective to positional power and the harm that this can bring to each of us.

Without the not-knowing stance, and the Speaker having a sense of their own presuppositions, there is a greater danger around power and control dynamics in any given conversation. Simply stated, if the Speaker thinks they are right in regards to their morality or their ethics, based on their presupposition of morality and ethics, they will be taking power and control in these conversations. The result is that the Speaker is setting themselves up to use Experiential Authority and potentially causing harm to the Listener.

For example, the Speaker may be having a conversation with someone who has just shared that they had an affair. In this example, some of the Speaker's presuppositions may be formed culturally and socially. North American society tends to frown on people having affairs and so the Speaker is influenced through the medium to think the same way. Therefore, one presupposition the Speaker may have is that affairs are wrong and because they are sitting in conversation with someone who had just told them that they had an affair, they are wrong and the Speaker is right.

This presupposition can be strengthened through culture. One cultural influence places a strong belief that if someone is in a relationship, it is with one person and that this relationship needs to remain monogamous. To have an affair would be to bring shame to the person's partner and would communicate their lack of worth and value to them. The irony in that statement is that because of the Speaker's own presuppositions, the Speaker would end up shaming the person who committed the affair. What the Speaker has done is not listened to the person who had the affair, but instead assigned a worth and value to them. The Speaker has imposed an External Identity with their associated measures of worth and value. If the person who had the affair was seeking a safe place to talk about and process what they have done, in a place of connection, the Speaker has in fact harmed them instead of helped.

In order for the person who had the affair to find any help out of a conversation, they would need to accept these imposing descriptions of worth and value from the Speaker before the connection can be established and the conversation continued. Through this process however, the person's self-descriptions of worth and value will continue to be defined through the Speaker. However, if the Speaker approached this conversation aware of their presuppositions around affairs they could introduce this through reflection and therefore minimize any harm that the Speaker would otherwise bring to the person who had the affair through the Speaker's use of Positional Authority. The idea here is that along with the Speaker's presuppositions comes an embedded sense of power and control. If the Speaker is not aware of their presuppositions, then they will also not be aware of how they are using power and control in conversation.

In addition, the Speaker may not be aware of how their non-verbals or verbal cues may be communicating a lack of worth or value to the Listener. Therefore, it is important that in conversation, the Speaker must assume they have presuppositions. The Speaker will then put the effort into recognizing what those presuppositions might be. More importantly, the Speaker will begin to wonder how those presuppositions may be influencing the conversation.

Something should be said about Experiential Authority now to shed some more light on what I will be talking about in this book. Experiential Authority is the language given to describe the imposed experience of the Speaker at the expense of the Listener's own experience. This External Identity will also come with embedded messages of worth and value that are accompanying that external experience from the Speaker. From an emotional point-of-view, after an encounter with Experiential Authority, the Listener normally experiences as a general feeling of grossness or yucky-ness. These experiences are described as a tendency to self-abase without really understanding why. The reason is that the Listener is feeling a lot of unlanguaged emotion around their encounter with the Speaker using Experiential Authority.

The focus of this book will be on the Listener's interaction and experience with Experiential Authority. In this context, I will attempt to define this new language of Experiential Authority and unpack it so the Listener can determine for himself or herself if it fits with their experience. Through this process of language discovery, I will endeavour to build an ever-increasing sense of self, addressing issues of External Identities and imposed meanings.

The idea is to help the Listener identify examples of where they may have run into Experiential Authority and to help them recognize the harm that it brings. However, through this process I will not offer up techniques on how the Listener may work to stop the Speaker from using Experiential Authority, as I view such things as frustrating and futile. Instead, I draw attention to the power differential that exists in Experiential Authority and through the naming of this experience; I surmise that the Listener will have a better sense of self. Therefore, I conclude that through the naming of Experiential Authority the

Listener will then be able to minimize the harm of its effects.

Hence, I have set out to introduce the language of Experiential Authority in hopes that my readers will feel empowered to try out that language on their experiences in order to see if it is a fit for them. I will then theorize if the language of Experiential Authority fits, then the naming of it, and understanding what it is, ends up removing the power behind it. The consequent naming of it will render its effects neutral, and allow the reader to maintain a healthy sense of self-worth and value.

I also observe that part of the Listener's susceptibility to Experiential Authority comes from a place of fear. Fear, in of itself is quite a powerful emotion and is only stripped of its power once the Listener has found other words to describe the fear. Once the Listener names the fear, it loses its power over them and they can process what is behind the fear. The challenge in naming this fear is that the fear the Listener is feeling is often accompanied by other emotions. These emotional experiences are often quite difficult for the Listener to process. It is my observation that most of the time the Listener tends to run away from, or minimize in some way, those emotional experiences that are full of pain and loss, thus making it more difficult to name the fear.

I suspect that at least one contributing factor to why this may be the case, is the tendency in our society to minimize the value of our emotional capacities. Instead, society elevates the worth of our cognitive capacities over our emotional capacities. The result is that the Listener struggles to find language to describe their emotions. To complicate this struggle the Listener tends to not associate as much worth and value to their emotions as they do to their cognition. Therefore, the Listener's emotions tend to remain speechless. The Listener is then highly susceptible to the Speaker who, from a place of Positional Authority, begins to invite the Listener to take on the Speaker's experience. All the while, the Speaker is asking the Listener to disregard their own experiences. The Listener then takes on the Speaker's External Identity, and along with it, descriptions of their own worth and value as described by the Speaker.

The reason the Listener tends to do this is that their own experiences may have woven throughout them stories of pain and loss. In the Listener's effort to minimize these emotions instead of seeking out language for them, they are initially attracted to the experience offered to them through the Speaker. This attraction is enhanced because it is being offered to the Listener without any stories of pain and loss attached to it. The Speaker may use the Listener's own stories of loss and pain in order to impose the Speaker's own experiences upon the Listener. From the Speaker's place of Positional Authority, they react to the Listener's experiences, perhaps defensively, but still with authority, which then places the Listener on the defensive. In other words, the Listener would end up defending their experiences to the Speaker.

What happens, however, is the Listener's unspoken emotional language is drawn out and attacked by the Speaker. Once the Listener responds to the Speaker defensively, the Speaker can then use Experiential Authority to impose an External Identity. This External Identity will come out of the Speaker's experience, which the Listener will take on as theirs, and along with it, the Speaker's own descriptions of the Listener's worth and value.

Over these past few years, I have come to call this process the Fear Perspective. This form of harm is amplified when the Speaker using the Fear Perspective is in a place of power and control, either through their position or through relation. When someone makes a statement regarding something the other person said, and that statement is corrective in nature, (i.e. "You should do … or this is wrong…") then there is a high probability that the statement is coming from a fear perspective. This fear perspective is simply fear without knowledge or understanding, which, when left unchecked can create misunderstanding and confusion.

Fear without knowledge or understanding seeks to inform itself through presuppositions and experiential knowledge. In the context of Experiential Authority, the Speaker does not take their experience and impose it upon the Listener but instead relates to the Listener from this Fear Perspective. What happens is the Speaker utilizes their Positional Authority to exert power and control over the Listener's experience by imposing a 'corrective' to their experience. It is as if the Speaker is saying, "Your experience is creating fear in me and because I am fearful of your experience I need you to change your experience or modify it in some way as to have it not create fear in me any longer." The Listener begins to doubt their experience and related values of identity, seeking instead to retreat or respond defensively. The result will be where the Listener would walk away from that conversation feeling gross or yucky inside, struggling with their unlanguaged emotional experience of that conversation.

Thus, Experiential Authority can be described as coming from a Fear Perspective. Experiential Authority becomes the construct of the Speaker's own experiences and presuppositions now imposed upon the Listener through a place of Positional Authority. The Speaker invites the Listener to disregard their own experiences of self and of what they have come to know as being right or true in their life. In that place, the Speaker invites the Listener to take on this External Identity presented to the Listener. The Listener, in turn, walks away from that interaction with feelings of grossness or yucky-ness, which slowly begins to erode their sense of value or self-worth. The Listener has replaced their own experience with the Speaker's and through that process, has minimized the identity of who the Listener is. The Listener is then drawn back to the Speaker in order to gain both a sense of self, along with a sense of their value and worth, only now those things are now defined through the Speaker.

Another very common use of Experiential Authority is something I have called Historical Relational Authority. Historical Relational Authority occurs when the Speaker who had some relationship with the Listener in the past is now relating to the Listener in the present through his or her descriptions of the Listener in the past. It surrounds the idea that the Listener does not change and is instead, defined by the Speaker, not by who the Listener is, but by what they did. The harm in this interaction is that the Speaker's sense of who the Listener *is* was based entirely on the Speaker's sense of who the Listener *was* in the past. The Speaker is constantly waiting to define the Listener by their view of who they thought the Listener was, instead of who the Listener is now. This also leaves the Listener feeling yucky and gross as they strive to remove those jackets of External Identities.

The antidote to these various ideas around Experiential Authority is an awareness of self and an understanding of the illusionary presence of power in relationships. From a place of healthy vulnerability, the Speaker can interact with the Listener from a not-knowing stance. From this place of not-knowing, space opens up in the conversation where the Listener can explore language to give voice to their emotional experiences. The Speaker can be aware of how their own stories of loss and pain have shaped them, while being reflective of their own presuppositions, and how those ideas may be influencing their participation in the conversation. Thus, the Speaker is working toward equalizing the power differential that may exist in various relationships. Finally, the Speaker can constantly be curious in their listening. Only then, does Experiential Authority lose its ability to harm, and instead leads the way into healthy, collaborative communities.

Chapter 2 My Brother's Suicide

July 10th 1990. 1:15pm. I was sitting on the edge of a cliff overlooking the Nicola Valley in British Columbia's Interior. This cliff was a few miles down a dirt road heading away from town, hugging the base of a mountain as it climbed higher and higher away from the valley below. At this particular corner in the road, it juts out, hanging over the Coldwater River a few hundred feet below. Given the narrowness of the dirt road this jut out was probably used by those old logging trucks as a space to allow vehicles to pass.

I had purposely chosen this place to become a Christian. I had travelled to this cliff side perch many times contemplating driving my car over the edge. It seemed like an ideal spot to do so, given its isolated location, the permanence of such an action, and the fact that there were already a handful of vehicles from decades past that lay in ruins at the bottom. The significance of this spot would not be lost on me, as a few years later I would return to this place with my brother's ashes and his widow by my side. However, my roommate was with me on this day, as he was instrumental in my decision to become a Christian.

One of my earliest childhood memories is of me sitting on my parent's sundeck in Courtenay, which is located on Vancouver Island, British Columbia. I was in grade four or five. My mother was teaching me about focusing and harnessing the energy within. She then taught me how to release it onto an object in order to create a reaction. In this case, the focus of that energy would be the few clouds that were in the sky. The sky was a brilliant blue, apart from those few clouds, and the sun was warm. This memory is quite vivid not because of the conversation with my mother but of the image that was created in my mind during that exercise.

I saw myself as this magnificently robed person, significantly older than I actually was, standing on top of a hill with an old oak tree as my backdrop. The sky was stormy, packed full of brilliant colors, red, orange, and yellow. Serving as a backdrop to these vivid colors was a blackness that filled every corner untouched by the storm. My mother instructed me to find the focal point in my mind to which the power in my body could be drawn to and 'harnessed'. Upon doing that, I was to envision this power slowly move down my arm and into my hand, where in a burst of cosmic and spiritual rays, this beam would extend out to the cloud in the sky, completely dissolving it on contact.

This image was intoxicating. I could feel the surge of power throughout my body and in my mind I was seeing lightning bolts, hearing thunder, and then seeing this ray beam of power shoot out of my body - all of which I had perfect control over. It was exhilarating. I was hooked and I wanted more. It did not bother me that it took at least half an hour for that cloud to be dissolved and it did not bother me to learn in science class a couple of years later that clouds would naturally dissolve quickly in certain atmospheric conditions. I had found my calling and I wanted this power so much that I decided to start pursuing it with a deep passion.

Over the next few years, I had many questions related to that experience. I wanted to understand how to do that again. I wanted to learn other techniques related to it. Other children may have collected rocks or stamps but my efforts were spent on collecting more and more of this knowledge. I was taught how to meditate, how to focus, how to go into a deeper state of meditation resulting in a trancelike state, how to harness power from your surroundings, and the list continued. I learned the power of crystals, the power of the mind, reincarnation, Rosicrucianism, self-healing the body, Transcendental Meditation, eastern religions including ancient Buddhism, and any other religion or practice of related interest.

Not entirely satisfied by what my quest had yielded thus far I started pursuing knowledge around mind control and manipulation techniques. This followed by a more spiritual focus, which resulted into the early stages of the occult. It was at this point that my family and I ended up moving to Merritt, British Columbia, which is located in the part of the province referred to as the Interior. This move came after about seventeen moves that my family had already gone through in my lifetime.

Although I now enjoy a wonderful relationship with my parents, at the time we were having typical teenage problems. I ended up leaving home when I was sixteen and returning to Kimberley, British Columbia, (the last place I just moved from). I had arranged to move in with my best friend's family, so after removing the back seat from my 1972 Dodge Dart Demon, I stuffed as many belongings as I could into this car and left home. Kimberley was where I deliberately started to involve myself with people associated with the occult.

I found employment at the local grocery store. I ended up rooming and boarding with a high-school teacher's family after a short time because of growing tensions with my friend's family. My life to this point now consisted of going to the gym six days a week, working, going to school, and drinking. When the town's main employer, the Cominco Mine, shut down, over one thousand families were out of work. People were walking into their banks and turning over the keys to their homes and vehicles.

Many people began to leave the community and I very quickly found myself without enough hours to pay for my own accommodations. Facing the prospect of no money to pay next month's expenses, I opted to leave Kimberley and return to Merritt. Having tasted what freedom was like, I did not want to stay at my parent's home, so I connected with a person I just met and we became roommates. I had gone back to the restaurant business and was now working full-time.

At first, I attempted to return to school, as I only had three months to graduation. However, showing up long enough to write an exam for English was not good enough for the teacher who told me that if I was not in every one of her classes until the end of the year that she would fail me. It did not seem to matter that I was scoring A's on her exams; she wanted to make an example out of me. Therefore, being the 'independent' person I was, I walked into the school office, told them what I thought about their English teacher, and I officially dropped out of High School.

Up to this point in my schooling, I had normally accomplished very high marks and was considered an academic achiever. Therefore, my decision to drop out of High School did not make a lot of sense for many people around me. I did not care, however, as I had become so consumed with anger toward so many people that I just wanted out. With bitterness fully taken root in my life, I walked out of that High School with a focus on work and when I was not working, self-destruction.

Unknown to me, my roommate was a very fervent Christian. His passion and dream was to become a Pastor and he was rarely without his twenty-pound, leather-bound, King James Version of the Bible. I wonder whether many a night he was on his knees praying for this cursing, drinking, and blasphemous roommate of his. My roommate was very involved in his local church and in particular the youth group. He would often have the youth group over to our apartment. As I was not there most of the time, I did not mind. I would grab a beer from my fridge, offer a polite hello and be on my way. However, it was during those few months with the youth group coming over to the apartment that really started to influence me.

This group of young people consistently showed unconditional love toward me, even at my worst, and that mystified me. I would curse and that would not stop them from talking and interacting with me. I would mock and they would continue to listen and care. It was not just that they continued to talk with me but it was how they talked. They showed me that they genuinely cared about me. They listened to my rants. They listened past my bad language and saw a hurt and wounded soul under it all. They loved me even when I hated myself and that confused me even more.

I started asking questions and they started sharing Bible stories with me. Up until that point, I had never heard of Jesus Christ or any of the Bible stories. I was drawn to everything I was hearing. I wanted to learn more about who Jesus was, more about the Bible, more about Christianity. How contrary this was to my spiritual background, however, there was a growing acknowledgment that what I was practicing was evil, even wrong, and I was being offered a way of wiping that slate clean.

Though I was ready to make a decision what finally convinced me of my immediate need to become a Christian was a girl who told me that she would not date a non-Christian. Suddenly the decision became very easy for me! Consequently, minutes after returning from that cliff-side conversion experience with my roommate, this girl and I began a relationship. Our relationship lasted a year and a half and ended up with me in a psych ward of a hospital down in the Lower Mainland of British Columbia. I had tried to kill myself by taking one hundred extra strength sleeping pills. My relationship with God was founded on my physical attraction to a girl and it did not get much deeper than that until I was released from the psych ward.

Upon my release from the psych ward, I immediately packed up everything I owned - which was not much – this time shoving it all into the back of my 1968 Ford van that was painted orange with house paint, and drove back to Merritt. I was now back home once again, picking up the pieces and starting over. I started attending the same church in which I became a Christian. At this point, I was just going through the motions hoping that I would 'bump into Jesus' along the way. I was lost, broken, disillusioned and full of unspoken questions.

I did not want to go to church that one particular Sunday morning in late fall but I did. I did not want to stay there after the service began but I did. At the end of the service an alter call was given and I did not want to go up but I did. One of the elders of the church came up to me and asked me want I wanted prayer for. I said I did not know but that I had try to kill myself just a few weeks earlier.

It was in this space that the most amazing life-changing event occurred. This man standing in front of me looked at me with tears in his eyes and hugged me. This was significant for me, as he was a prominent businessperson in the community and was at least twice my size. He did not pray one word but just stood there hugging me. At that moment, I experienced what I compassionately refer to as "a hug from God". It felt that the entire church disappeared and I was standing in the presence of a bright light. This elder was gone and there standing in front of me was Jesus. He just stood there hugging me and I felt for the first time in my life and definitely the first time since I had become a Christian over a year and a half earlier that I was truly loved of God.

Through the experience of interacting with the youth in my apartment, and now this experience at the alter I began to understand the importance of worth and value. In particular, how worth and value transcended our ability to measure them both and define them, which had been my experience in the past. I felt challenged to begin looking at others in this same way. I came to understand that to measure people's worth and value in relation to their experiences, what they say, or even what they look like, is wrong, and that they have an intrinsic worth and value that goes beyond those measurements. In other words, their worth and value cannot be measured by anything we can imagine and that their worth and value comes from their just being. These early experiences, standing as a deep contrast to my old spiritual life and experiences, served as a catalyst in how I interacted with people moving forward.

Two weeks after this Sunday morning experience changed my life, I met the girl who in a few years would become my wife. We had met through the youth group earlier but nothing formally, although we somewhat knew of the other person. In fact, our paths had crossed a couple of ways in those first two years of me being a Christian. We ended up being the only two youth that were baptized on a particular Sunday in October. The second and perhaps humorous way was that she ended up dating my girlfriend's younger brother for a while. Within a few months of my return to Merritt, we were dating, and shortly after that, we knew we were going to marry each other. Three years later we did.

I have a younger brother. Two years younger in fact. He became a Christian in December of 1990. Afterwards, I was wondering if Kyle had been sincere in his decision or not because it appeared as though nothing had changed. I often wondered if his desire to say a prayer was more for my sake than his. When he became a Christian, I gave him a white leather-bound Bible. It had a multi-colored stranded bookmark and I was particularly proud of that purchase for him. It would be several years later when I realized that this Bible was not the same as mine as it contained the Deuterocanonical and Apocryphal Books.

He lived in the same city as me but we rarely saw one another as we travelled in different social circles. At the time, we both had our issues with our parents and we both had our issues with each other. A few years later, he got married and although he still lived in the same community, it was if he disappeared altogether. I would seem him from time to time but we could not really connect with one another. I suppose that I disappeared from him as well, as I had gotten married by now, and was beginning a new family with my wife's and my first child on the way.

On May 5th, 1997, I was able to get a hold of my brother and set up a time that we could talk. He had been quite heavy on my heart over the previous few weeks and I wanted to connect with him. We would see each other occasionally but most of the time it was a hit and miss situation. This time I needed to say some things to him that were troubling me. I was struggling with how to introduce the topic and to find the words to share. We agreed that he would meet me at my work at 11pm. I was finishing closing up the restaurant when he pulled up in his pick-up truck. He got into my car so we could go for a drive. Very quickly into the drive, I apologized to him for how I had been treating him and his wife. I was concerned that I had been too judgmental of their relationship and as a result that I had hurt them and pushed them away. I shared with him that I felt that he was hurting and I was wondering if he might be feeling very depressed.

This meeting was all the more important to me because his marriage had recently fallen apart only a few months after they had been married. Although they had cohabitated for quite a while without any noticeable relationship concerns, it seemed as though soon after they were married, any problems lurking under the surface were exposed for others to see. He moved out in the midst of some accusations that his wife was being unfaithful to him and engaging in a lesbian relationship. Within a few years of their separation, his wife had taken in a female roommate, which after several more years of them living together they were married. This seemed to confirm people's suspicions that perhaps my brother's accusations had been correct all along.

My heart felt very heavy that night as I talked with him and I decided that I would be bolder and more directive in my conversation. I took a leap and proceeded to let him know that I felt he might be suicidal and that I was worried about him. He was silent and in those moments, I grew uncomfortable with the silence so I continued. I shared a bit about what God had done for me in this area of suicidal thoughts and that I wanted to make myself available to him if he needed to talk. I told him that he was very valuable to me, that I appreciated him as a brother, and that I did not want anything to happen to him.

He was emotionless throughout the conversation. He was distant from me and his only response was the constant referring to two gold rings that he found on the seat of his truck just prior to coming up to the restaurant. It was as if I was not there at all. It was if he had already made the decision. As our drive ended, I realized how late it was getting and found myself wanting to drop him off quickly so I could get home to my wife and child. I ended the conversation and left him standing alone in that dark parking lot. As I drove off, I looked in my rear-view mirror to see him very slowly opening the door to his truck and getting in. That was the last time I ever saw him.

The next night at work, I received a phone call. It was approximately 8pm.

"Good evening. Michael speaking. How can I help you?"

"...Mike..."

"...Mom!?..."

"Ah...I have some...news...bad news..."

"What's wrong?"

"Ah..."

"Mom!? What's wrong?"

"Are you sitting down?"

"I just did. What's wrong? What's going on?"

"I have some bad news..."

"What is it!? What's wrong!?"

"Kyle is dead..."

The stool I was sitting on slammed against the counter behind me. All strength instantly drained from my entire body. My six-foot frame was desperately clinging to a three-foot countertop, as if I was hanging from the top of a cliff. Clutching the phone desperately, my glasses half-cocked on my face and my eyesight blurred by a wall of tears I stammered into the phone.

"...Wwhat?"

"The officer is here with dad. Do you want them to come get you...?"

"...Wwhat?"

"They will be there in five minutes...Dad has to go to the hospital...Is this alright?"

"...ok..."

"Ok. Bye..."

"...bbye..."

Gathering what strength was left in my body I rose to my feet and in a complete daze, I staggered outside to a patio table. I felt as if I was bleeding uncontrollably. My chest heaved with such an intense pain as inside a knot twisted and turned. I was convulsing with every teardrop. I found it very difficult to breathe. I lost all my strength in my legs. There was no feeling - nothing. I was reduced to a one month old who was struggling to figure out what was going on around them. My head would spin and then stop suddenly, throbbing rhythmically.

Everything was out of control. I lost my grip on reality and I was stuck somewhere between reality and insanity. It was so difficult to breathe. The pain hurt like nothing I had ever imagined; nothing any horror movie could ever come close to recreating. What has happened? What was going on? Kyle? I could not think about that without wanting to scream. I could not scream. I could not do anything. I was completely helpless. I was lost in the blackness of space. NOOOOOOOO! It was the night before that we had talked. A good talk I thought. A beginning. The end.

Still in a daze, I had not noticed that my wife had driven up as per normal as she was picking me up before we went and picked up our daughter. She had not yet been informed of what had happened. Our daughter had been left with a sitter earlier in the evening. Seeing me in obvious distress, my wife came running over with tears already in her eyes asking what was wrong. I barely managed to utter a couple of words, which did not make any sense at all, but was enough to cause complete panic in Jasmine.

Being a new mother and seeing me in distress brought a wave of fear and through our broken conversation with each other; she thought that our daughter had died. Complete hysteria broke out with the both of us as I was trying to tell her that it was in fact my brother and not our daughter. In a terrifying few minutes, I was granted momentary sanity to help pull my wife together and explain to the best of my knowledge what had happened. My wife went completely into shock still worrying about Hellen and not grasping what had happened with Kyle. I told her that I was waiting for the police and for her to go and get our daughter. Reluctantly she left, still sorting out all the facts.

Out of the darkness came the headlights of the police car. It had been twenty minutes and not the five like my mother had said. The waiting drove me to desperation. After my wife left, I found myself looking around frantically in the dark for something or someone. I was incredibly angry, completely devastated, and very confused. I looked out into the parking lot with the only light coming from within the restaurant. Just the night before Kyle had been there in his truck. He got into my car and we had gone for a long drive and a long talk. I dropped him off and watched him get into his truck as I drove away. What had happened? I needed the facts. NO! It cannot happen that way! Why that way?! This is not fair! NO!

"If it is any consolation it was painless..."

"He just lied down and went to sleep..."

My brother loved to go four-wheel driving. In Merritt there is a popular spot used by a variety of outdoor enthusiasts referred to as the Flats. The terrain starts with a series of moguls and through a trail of winding roads, it eventually gives way to the mountains. It was here that my brother decided to go; to the place he loved. In a small section of the flats, there is a series of smaller hills lying at the base of the mountain. A water tower once stood about halfway up one of these small hills. This area is well guarded by all the trees and undergrowth. Only the foundation remains with some twisted metal lying in decay from decades of neglect. At one time, this water tower stood tall and proud, providing its life-giving contents to all the inhabitants below. After outliving its usefulness, the water tower was dismantled for scrap, leaving behind only little clues as to what it once was.

When you are down below looking up, this place is lost in the vegetation and trees. The only clue, which points the way, is a perfectly straight line of power poles making its way up to the water tower. At the last pole, the wires still hang there lifelessly with nothing to connect to. Standing at this site and looking down you are able to see the entire valley bottom in which Merritt is located. How majestic a view and in another time this would have made a peaceful, tranquil spot for a picnic. I smiled, not in a humorous way, but in the way when you all of a sudden understand what was going on. I had my cliff and Kyle had his water tower.

"He lied down and just went to sleep..."

"If it's any consolation; it was painless..."

Kyle had put a lot of thought into what he had done. He did not warn anybody the night before; he just did it. It seemed like he had talked about suicide no more and no less than anyone else did, and to his friends he was a rock, their rock. Quite often, if someone were feeling down, it would be Kyle who they would go to. No one really missed Kyle at work that day, since it was quite common for people not to show up at all for a variety of reasons. Kyle had his share of them.

He was not wearing his wedding ring. He had taken that off two and a half months earlier. The same day he packed his belongings and left his home, that wedding band remained behind on the dresser. In the cab of the truck, they also found his cell phone. The battery was dead which indicates that it had been on. Was someone going to call him? Was he going to call someone? Those questions and feelings continued to haunt me for years. I should have called him. I was the last person to talk to him the previous night. It took me several years to work through that guilt.

In his note, there were a couple of paragraphs for me. In it, he had told me not to feel guilty because it was not my fault.

In fact, he went on to say he was so encouraged by our talk the night before that he almost decided against this choice. Almost?! This proved to be the hardest of items to deal with. I would always hear the accusations whispered in my ear as I thought about this. "You let him down once again. He was relying on you to help him and you put your needs before his." It would be several years of finding safe people to talk to about my brother, before I could process many of my painful emotions around his death.

Chapter 3 My Suicide Attempt

It was twelve noon and the phone still had not rung. The day was Monday, October 28, 1991, my brother's birthday. I had been lying beside the phone all morning waiting for it to ring. Hesitantly, I got up, grabbed my keys and wallet and began what I had intended to be my final journey.

I was living in Langley, British Columbia at the time. Back in September, my girlfriend and I had packed everything we owned into my 1968 Ford van and started out for university in Langley. During that summer, she was living in Kelowna with her parents and I was the unwelcome guest. I had spent the last month and a half of summer living in my van on the beaches around Kelowna. I would wait until late night to sneak my van onto some beach and then try hard to wake up before any patrols would come by. I was not always successful and it became a bit of a game by the end of those few weeks.

I would spend my time furiously trying to finish the last two courses I needed in order to graduate and be eligible for university. Since I had not worked on these two courses since dropping out of high school a year and a half earlier I was running out of time. To help me accomplish this huge goal, my girlfriend offered to complete my English course while I focused on my geography course. I would spend my days working out of my van with the Okanagan Lakes as my backdrop, furiously trying to finish all of my assignments. I would take breaks, long enough to sneak into my girlfriend's house when her parents were not there to have a shower and a bite to eat before picking up her completed assignments.

Just days before the University deadline to submit my transcripts I had managed to finish my last two high school courses. I had done well in both my English course and my Geography course. Writing the provincial exam for my Geography course was simply enough but I remember staring blankly at much of my English provincial exam. In those terrifying few moments I realized that perhaps my strategy to finish on time by using my girlfriend to complete my English course was not a good idea. Fortunately, my girlfriend was very good at English so I was able to squeak out a C for the course even though I failed my provincial exam.

By the time we were driving down to Langley, I had spent my last few dollars on the gas in my van. My only asset was my microwave bouncing around in the back. In retrospect, it was fair to say that the only reason why I was going to university was that she was. I arrived on campus with fumes in my tank. I think deep down I knew that I was not going to get my student loan. I wanted to try for it anyway as an excuse to leave home, leave the town, and the people. I felt that making this move would strengthen my relationship with my girlfriend and fix my problems. I was wrong.

I was running from my past and this was a race I was about to lose. I entered this new world broke, depressed, and spiritually unstable. I wondered how it was that I was now at a Christian university when I did not really know what it meant to be a Christian. Within the first week of class, I had found out that my loan was not approved. I had chosen not to go to any classes and instead take advantage of the cafeteria food until the school administration found out. My roommate did not question why I was skipping classes or why I was only half-unpacked, keeping most of what I owned in my van. I quickly found a buyer for my last asset and used those fifty dollars to put as much gas in my tank as possible.

As a matter of survival, I needed to find a job, and I knew that it was only a matter of time before the university would question my living there. I quickly found a job at a local restaurant. This restaurant belonged to the same chain that I had worked for back in Merritt. When I walked into the restaurant and asked the owner for a job, I was pleasantly surprised to have them share that they were waiting for me to show up. As it turned out, my previous employer called them and gave a glowing reference. I was hired as the newest member of their management team and began immediately.

On my first shift, I ran into a family that I had met in Merritt several months earlier through a mutual friend. During the conversation with them, they offered me a room in their home at no charge. Imagine, in a couple of days I had a place to stay with free room and board and a full time job! Things were looking up for me in this new place and I was looking forward to the future. However, in the weeks after I had left the university campus, my relationship with my girlfriend fell apart. It seemed as though for my girlfriend, this was her first taste of freedom and the attention she was receiving from all the guys flattered her. She found herself falling for another guy and in her guilt was trying to cover it up. This other guy was studying to become a youth pastor and he did not seem to mind that she was already in a serious relationship.

He pursued her and in the process introduced her to marijuana. She experimented with it and became a serious practical joker pulling off some dangerous stunts. I went into a jealous rage and started into a downward spiral of depression. During the month prior to my suicide attempt, all I could talk about, think about, and pray about, was suicide. In subtle ways, I started searching for someone to listen to me or to care; I found neither. My feelings were becoming too intense to control.

On one particular evening, I had gone to see my girlfriend at the campus. It was then when I found out that she was cheating on me and through her roommates, found out she wanted to end our relationship. I went back to my van and began smashing it with my fists. I ripped off the antenna and began to tear apart the interior. It was a dark and foggy evening and as I pounded the van into gear, racing out of the campus parking lot, I am not sure how I managed not to smash into another vehicle. I got onto the highway heading back to the city, completely oblivious to anything else. In a state of complete hysteria, I yanked the wheel sharply to the left entering the oncoming lane, and after crossing the lane, the van left the road.

It smashed down on a gravel area and not being dead I put the gear into park. Stumbling out of the van I looked around, trying to see where I was. When the fog lifted, I found that I had landed in a very small gravel pullout on the side of the road, surrounded by marsh. In my frustration with being so inadequate in my attempt to end my life I dejectedly returned to my van and drove myself home. Something needed to break and still I could not find any help.

Finally, on a Sunday evening, I told a few co-workers that if I did not receive a phone call by noon the following day that I was going to kill myself. I was feeling quite low that evening and was responsible for closing the restaurant. Several employees also stayed around, offering a hand in the closing. When I told these employees what I was planning, only a couple offered some advice, while the others ignored my emotional rants altogether.

Getting into my van at noon the next day, after the phone still had not rung, provided me with more courage to continue with the plan. I had thought this through with the same intensity matching my rage and I now knew what to do. Each drugstore I stopped at my stories became more and more convincing. They were stories of sleep disorders, bad dreams, lack of sleep, no sleep in days, and the list went on. I bought extra strength, the biggest boxes, and whatever else I thought would help make this successful.

An hour and five drugstores later I was back at home in my room. One hundred pills, some blue, most white, were in a pile beside me on the bed. I had a glass of water on the nightstand, which was not too full since I did not want to dilute the poison. I looked at the pills and then at the phone. Why did the phone not ring?

The note was finished and placed neatly on the bed where they would find it. I sat on the edge of the bed and stared at the door. Their children would not be home until four and I was not expecting the parents until later that night. This gave me lots of time to swallow the pills and have them take effect. In my desperation, I started to cry but my anger and consuming hatred of everything around me quickly dried up the tears. Who cares anyway? I EVEN TOLD THEM!

I stared blankly at the wall in front of me. Darkness surrounded me and a barrier separated me from God. I started to pray. "Lord..." No, no I do not think I said that. My prayer was not really a prayer as it was more just me clearing my conscience. "Jesus I can't see you, feel you or hear you. You are so far away from me. Just blackness. I tried. I am sorry. I do not know what is going to happen now. I do not want to go to hell. I hope you will be there when I die..."

The first one was the hardest. It must have taken me five minutes to swallow that little blue pill. It took me another five minutes to swallow the other ninety-nine and I still had half of the water left in my glass. After swallowing the last pill, I turned my head and stared at the wall again.

"Well it's done. Now I guess I wait." In a matter of seconds, I experienced what felt like a hand reaching from across the room, gripping me, and throwing me to the floor. I felt my eyes roll to the back of my head and everything started to cloud over. Someone or something was trying to pull my brain out of my head.

I must have weighed two thousand pounds as I strained to raise my head off the carpet. I was determined not to die from suffocation. I was going to die from sleeping. I wanted to get back onto the bed but I could not move. I began to gag. I remember thinking that I could not throw up or it would not be successful.

Ohhhh! Out came a lot of water and some yellow liquid. Again, I was thinking that it would be successful since it was not a lot of the pills. Ow! Let go of me! Something grabbed hold of me and began to pull me; pulling me into myself like a vacuum sucking from your inside. The last thing I remember was that I needed to get some paper towel to clean up the mess I just made...

This scene has replayed itself in my

mind repeatedly since that day. I have spent many sleepless nights dealing with all the feelings that I was experiencing. I have often wondered about the circumstances leading up to them finding me. By the grace of God, the parents came home early. They looked in on me and found me lying on the bed with the phone hanging off the hook. This scene bothered me. How did I get back onto the bed? Had someone tried to call me? Did I try to call someone?

The next twenty-four hours is patchy. I was in and out and when I was awake, I was hallucinating. I was not wearing any clothes and wires were stuck all over me. I felt like I was strapped to the bed. I probably was. Every thirty seconds an automatic pump would squeeze my arm. Every thirty seconds I feared my heart was going to explode. A black tar-like substance, which tasted like gravel mixed with molasses, was forced down my throat.

Having never used drugs of any sort, I was not familiar with hallucinations. With what was happening to me in reality being weird enough the combination of the hallucinations really messed me up. In fact, they were powerful enough to create confusion for me as to what was real or not for the next couple of days. Lying on this bed, surrounded by curtains, and a large bright light over me, did not help with the hallucinations either.

As I took in what was going on around me I gazed outside through a huge picture window into a lonely snow-covered parking lot. There parked by a tree was my van. Funny, I had not remembered driving myself to the hospital. Looking beside my bed, I was shocked to see my brother sitting there with his girlfriend sitting on his lap. Kyle was fast asleep and it looked like his girlfriend was falling asleep as well. I said hello, but neither answered me. I called out their names but I was still ignored. I continued to yell at them for some time until suddenly they disappeared. At that moment, the pump started again and I blacked out.

I woke up the next afternoon. I was in a brightly lit room with five other hospital beds. I was wearing a gown. I was disorientated, confused, and afraid.

"Where am I?" I asked the nurse who just walked in.

"Langley," she said.

I became desperate knowing that this nurse served as my only connection to reality at this time.

"Are you sure?" I questioned.

"Yes. You came in yesterday afternoon. This is the psychiatric wing of the Langley hospital. You were moved here out of emergency late last night."

At that moment, another nurse came into the room asking for her assistance.

"I'll be right back. I need to ask you some questions."

She placed down the papers she had with her on a table by my bed and left with the other nurse. After she was gone, I quickly grabbed the papers. I needed to know if she was telling me the truth or not. I was still thinking that I had gotten into my van, drove to the Merritt hospital and was there. Why else would my brother and his girlfriend be there?

Every page of these papers had a Langley hospital stamp on it. I looked around this empty room in desperation. There was a window in the room but instead of glass, there were glass blocks, which allowed light in, but you could not look out. I sat on the edge of my bed with my head resting in my arms. "Oh man. I have no idea what is going on or where I am."

That was probably one of the longest weeks of my life. Sitting in a room across from people that had tried to end their lives, some more than once, was not an easy place to be. Their stories were hard, angry, and full of hopelessness. I felt like a foreigner in a strange country. I should not be in this place. This was not me. Sadly, though, it was. My story was no different from theirs. Every day of that week, I spent every available opportunity convincing the staff that I was okay to be released. I think they finally let me go out of desperation for another bed. A guy was just brought in for trying to slit his wrists after breaking up with his girlfriend. I

Page | 55

knew how he felt.

The family that I was staying with was gracious enough to let me return to their home. It was eerie being in the same room once again, it felt so dark and cold. I gathered up my possessions and once again loaded them into my van. When I went to the restaurant to let them know where I had been for the last couple of weeks I was met with the same coldness and the door. Losing my job reminded me of all my losses as I now found myself without a home or a future. Broken, lost, confused, and feeling as if my future was bleak, I filled up my gas tank with the few dollars I had left, and started back on the highway heading toward the Interior of British Columbia.

I was nervous about returning to Merritt. I had brought humiliation and disappointment to my parents and I had tried to kill myself on my brother's birthday. I did not know if I could look any of them in the face again. This journey of my suicide attempt brought me to that Sunday morning in which I was released from the demons that plagued me. The shame was washed away. My personal demons were chased off, and in the brilliant light that replaced the darkness stood Jesus. Even though many relationships were broken, and I was once again picking up the pieces, I had a peace that gave me strength to go on.

Here is a story I wrote around fifteen years ago, sometime after I had lost my brother, as I pondered life and my relationship with everything around me. My relationship to others and to life itself has always fascinated me, at first to try to control it, and now, later in life, with how to embrace and enjoy it.

The dew soaked ground shimmered as the morning rays burst forth from the clouds above and splashed its warmth upon the ground. Autumn colored leaves dropped to the earth beneath taking their time along the way.

A beautiful web sparkled from the sunlight as a spider scurried from the old rusted can at one end of the web to the old tired fence at the other end. Along the top of the fence, a little grey mouse ran along stopping suddenly every few feet to glance around.

The scene was silent with the only sound coming from a light wind rustling through some tall blades of grass. From over the top of the hill in the distance, a little boy came running up alongside the fence. Behind the boy, was his dog barking and jumping about. He was laughing and running a stick along the pickets of that old fence which made a clicking sound as he ran.

Over by an old tree, the little boy stopped and sat down. His dog ran up beside him and gratefully lay down panting heavily. The little boy looked over the countryside beneath him and picking up a few stones tossed a few to nowhere in particular.

Before his eyes, the winds began to chance. Different colors mixed in the sky above and like an illusion, the countryside began to roll, changing shape like clay in the potter's hands. Far below this little boy could see his town taking shape in a different way.

It was growing; creeping up the hillside toward him. Every few seconds a burst of flame would erupt from the town but then it was if even a newer building would emerge from the fire. Slowly new homes, roads and subdivisions emerged from the hillside as the land gave birth to all of it.

Not only was his town changing but also now, the land around the little boy started to change. The old fence decayed to a point of disrepair, long-time covered with growth. The little boy looked down at his dog, which looked back with love and innocence in its eyes. It started to age in front of this boy while melting into this hypnotic backdrop.

He saw himself and his parents standing over a crude cross, stuck into the ground behind a mound of dirt. They all had tears in their eyes and hugged each other for comfort until they too disappeared into the background.

Down below the town was still growing. Now he could sense that he himself was changing; getting older - no longer a little boy but now a teenager, no - a young man. Then from this ever-changing backdrop, a beautiful young woman emerged and placed her hand in his. He was not shocked by this action as it seemed natural and part of what was going on.

There they both sat side by side still watching the landscape change around them and with it themselves. A ring appeared on both of their hands and they sat a bit closer. Out to their left a subdivision was making its way toward them and finally at the end of a cul-de-sac, a house appeared. Behind this green house was a swing set and a sandbox.

At this point, the sky returned to normal and the evening sun was dipping below the horizon. From the rear of the house, a little child appeared and started running toward this couple with a little puppy in tow. "Mommy, Daddy!" she laughed as the little puppy barked happily at her heels.

The little girl sat down at her parent's feet and picked up some stones. Her puppy ran up and gratefully lied down, panting heavily. The little girl then took her stones and started throwing them to nowhere in particular.

The significance of this story was that it was never me. I moved so often that it has become a way of life. If I saw all four seasons in one location, I counted myself fortunate. This story became a way for me to reflect on what could have been and what was lost. Perhaps this is the draw to have the Listener take on the experience of the Speaker. Perhaps this is the reason why the Listener can so easily dismiss his or her own experiences for the sake of the Speaker's experience. Perhaps it is because the Listener's own experiences contain loss, trauma, hurt, and pain, which they tend to want to avoid, deny, and dismiss. Perhaps then, the experience offered by the Speaker is idealistic in its nature.

Like my story above, the Speaker offers the Listener an experience, describing a place the Listener only dreamed of, and more important, without the reminders of their own loss and pain. The Listener is drawn to this place, a place without loss or pain, without any reminders of their own hurts. Consequently, the experience presented by the Speaker becomes something that the Listener wants, but after they have taken it, the experience becomes empty and imposing.

This transaction of receiving the Speaker's experience at the expense of the Listener's happens quite quickly. It happens so quickly in fact that the space to explore the Listener's own emotions, and in particular their related stories of loss, is not very large. The idea of taking space in order to explore the Listener's own emotions is not a popular one because the Listener is conditioned through popular culture, media, and social constructs that emotional expressions need to fit into particular times and places.

The Listener trips and struggles over their own stories of loss, devaluing them in the process, because of these external ideologies. The Listener hears messages around them that if they do not deal with *it* and press on they will be left behind. An anxiety sets in and the Listener's focus becomes on minimizing or trading in their pain and loss for something ideal and socially acceptable.

How blindly the Listener then reaches out and embraces what is offered to them. The Listener overlooks the fact that what is being offered to them is idealistic and more reflective of what they really want then what really is. The External Identity that the Listener grabs on to comes at a cost. The Listener believes, initially, that what they have replaced their own experiences with would make them happy, fulfilled, and joyful even.

However, the reality is that these descriptions of fulfillment, joy, and happiness, do not reflect this External Identity. Instead the Listener is faced with having their worth and value defined by the Speaker. The Listener is at the mercy of the Speaker and as a result, the Listener loses the sense of who they really are. The Listener has lost the chance to find language to describe their emotional experience. This is because instead of listening and exploring their own emotions, the Listener traded them in for the Speaker's experience.

It is in this in-between place of embracing the experience presented to the Listener that they fall victim to Experiential Authority, because they are running from their own pain and loss. Could the Listener's susceptibility to these External Identities be born out of a desperate hope that what they take on would somehow be better than what they have? Is the Listener's ease in dismissing their own experiences a result of not understanding their worth and value in spite of their circumstances?

Worth and value, as an ideal that is pursued like a sunken treasure, hold so much power in our society. Those with the power define worth and value, offering a measurement of it. However, when the Listener attempts to measure worth and value, it becomes an experiential measuring of something that is used to define who they are. This is the problem with External Identities through Experiential Authority because they come with imbedded measurements of worth and value. The Listener is told that because of their circumstances, or their pain/loss, their worth and value has diminished as well.

However, one of the ideas being presented in this book is that each of us have an intrinsic worth and value that goes beyond anyone's attempt to measure it. Therefore, not simply in spite of one's pain, loss and circumstances does one have worth and value but in addition to one's pain, loss and circumstances. This idea of adding in one's pain and loss as part of the equation into our own worth and value seems ludicrous in a society that goes to great lengths to avoid such things.

How can the Listener have an immeasurable worth and value if their own experiences are littered with sorrow, pain, loss, and trauma? The Listener hears their own painful stories echoing in their head, beating upon their chest, and just for a moment, they listen to the wonderful words coming from the Speaker. The Speaker captivates the Listener with what the Speaker is saying and for a moment, the Listener forgets themself, long enough to take on an External Identity. In that brief moment it has been long enough to be lost to who they are, desperately seeking a worth and value that transcends the experiences they have lived.

This is a tremendous hurdle to overcome, this idea of understanding one's own worth and value in spite of or in addition to one's circumstances. This makes the Speaker's offer more attractive because the experience they are inviting the Listener to take on comes with no pain and no loss. Although the idea of having an experience that seems to remove one's own pain and loss is attractive to many, the result will end up perpetuating the existing messages of worthlessness and devaluing. These messages of worthlessness are perpetuated because the Listener's own voices and their own experiences have not been heard nor validated.

It was painful living a life full of depression and despair. Constantly I would come to a cliff and ponder jumping off or driving off. I would find myself in many circumstances that I would consider killing myself. As early as those memories in Courtenay, I would wonder what it would be like if I threw myself in front of a passing train. My life was entwined with thoughts of suicide. I became very angry with everyone and everything around me. It was painful sitting on the edge of that bed on that

Monday afternoon not-knowing what it would be like if I did not exist. All I knew was that I did not want to exist. In that moment, I had no sense of my own intrinsic worth and value. This would come later.

Chapter 4 The Birth of Experiential Authority

These early experiences and certainly my decision to become a Christian, walking away from an occult-based spirituality, were instrumental and foundational in how I began to look at life around me. In particular, it was the early encounters with an unconditional love that I am often drawn back to. In my work with Experiential Authority and consequent research around relational dynamics, I have often explored this idea of unconditional love and the power that it has in of itself.

It could have been said that the youth who were in my shared apartment, visiting my bible-thumping roommate, were there to proselytize me. Perhaps there was some truth in that, but there was something unusual in their conversations. I felt like I had a worth and a value when I was around them. This was a different sense of worth and value, one that was not performance-based, or academically-based, as if I figured out the right answer. Even though I would mock them and curse them, it did not seem to matter. Not all of my conversations were faith-based and in the midst of those conversations, I felt listened to. There was an equalization of power in the relationships and this confused me.

This confusion was the result of my own earlier religious experiences. My focus on gaining power through exerting control over others was a common theme of my religious disciplines. I was learning how to manipulate, how to control, and how to have power. I dedicated much of my daily routine and life to this pursuit and would relish in the little victories along the way. I would grow relentless in my pursuit of power but given its illusionary aspects, I would constantly be frustrated in my efforts to hold onto it for any great amount of time.

Now, I was in a room of peers who did not seem concerned about power. They made no mention of it nor did they indicate through their actions that they were in pursuit of it. Instead, all that was present was a focus on communicating worth and value to me, creating space for me to talk, and then listening to me. They seemed genuinely interested in what I was saying and there was a curiosity on their part with what I was saying. They asked for clarification and sought to understand my experience of what I was sharing. Out of these conversations, and many others like it, came the various ideas that I have developed around power and authority in relationships.

In the first year and a half of being a Christian, I was wrestling with what it meant to be a Christian, who God was, and who I was in relationship to God. My own suicide attempt was an agonizing journey of trying to understand my own worth and value against a backdrop of harmful relationships and various misuses of power and authority. It also characterized the struggle of understanding the idea that He was God and I was not. My previous spiritual pursuits falsely exalted self over others and so quite often I would glance down from my arrogant heights, examining the wretchedness of those around me. I would seek out ways to manipulate and control, completely oblivious to the fact that in my pursuit of power I was powerless.

When I became a Christian I was not only depressed and suicidal, I was exhausted. I had spent so much of my adolescent years seeking to detach from my own pain and loss, never to escape its reality. It was not enough for me to hear and read what my relationship with God was supposed to look like; I needed to explore my own emotional journey. I needed to find both the space and the language to express the pain and the loss.

I suspect that as a result of these emotional experiences from my past, which I was trying to sort out, contributed to why I had invited the pastor of the church I was attending at the time, up to my place of work for a coffee. Coincidently, this conversation ended up being only a few short months before my brother committed suicide. I knew what I wanted to do when I invited my pastor to my workplace but I had no idea on how to say it. When he showed up I invited him to take a seat and then I started to talk.

"I feel that I need to do something that I have never done in my life and I don't quite understand why I need to do this, only that I feel God wants me to do this." With that statement, I went on to explain that I needed to have accountability in my life, which meant that I needed to come under his pastoral leadership. I needed to make myself accountable to him and this meant that I needed to submit to his leadership even if that came into my personal life.

As I reflect on that initial conversation, I am struck at how much I focused on the language of need. This was not a want or a desire but I felt that something was lacking from my life. In hindsight, as I was searching for words to express my pain and loss, I reflected on my lack of language to communicate that pain and loss. I was exploring my emotions from a vulnerable place and in my effort to be a better Christian I responded with the language of need. I find it interesting now to look back and see how I had equated need to an obedience of 'doing' what was right. It would seem that I was seeking a worth and value through the measurement that best fit my experience and that measurement was through performance.

I felt good about what I was doing while at the same time I did not fully understand what it was I was doing either. What I mean is that for the next two years I hated the very thing I just did. I could not believe that I would have been so silly as to enter into such a covenant with my pastor. Imagine! I just gave the pastor an open invitation to challenge me in every area of my life! Every day I regretted that decision and I told him so. He would just smile back and tell me that he loved me and that was it. In those two years, it seemed like he did not take advantage of this power that I had given him. I was vulnerable and in much pain, yet he just came alongside my life at certain times and pointed out the obvious. Because I had made this decision to submit to his authority, I listened.

Several times over those two years, I would say I could not stand him. It seemed he was always right! Why did I make this decision? Why did I feel like I needed to do this? This was such a difficult time for me as I wrestled with my relationship with God as it was entwined with my relationship with this pastor. Over the course of those two years, the pastor and I became good friends. We would end up spending a bunch of time together, attending different events and through the course of those two years, I felt that I had gained both a mentor and a friend. It was common for us to share some laughs and even tears together. This relationship was a great support to me as I continued to grow in my relationship with God while he continued to support me.

It seemed, though, that my wife benefited the most during this two years. God had done a lot of work in my life to make me into the man, the husband, and the father that I needed to be, and it seemed like my wife was thanking God on a daily basis. Because of the accountability-relationship that I was in, I could no longer do things or say things to my wife without that pastor coming into my life to bring loving and gentle correction.

Let me illustrate this with something

that happened at a church meeting. This was a business meeting and in addition to discussing other agenda items, we were there to discuss and then approve the budget. As the pastor was presenting the budget for the upcoming year, he was challenging the membership to accept what he had called a faith budget. In other words, the amount of income and expenses was considerably higher than our average income and the pastor's challenge to us was to rise up in faith and support this budget.

I found myself quite angry about this but could not explain why. At the end of the meeting, I picked up my daughter and stormed out of the church with my daughter in my arms. On the way outside, I had unknowingly bumped my daughter's head into the door of the church. It was enough for her to start crying and try to tell me that I had just bumped her head. I was not paying attention, as all I wanted to do was to leave that place. A couple of days later my pastor came to see me. He commented that it seemed that I was quite upset at the business meeting and wondered if I wanted to talk about that. I tried to brush it off and told him that I did not want to talk about it. I was still too upset and could not find the words to express why or even what about.

He then looked at me and told me when I had left the church I had bumped my daughter's head on the door. He explained that she tried to tell me what had happened but I did not pay attention. He then went on to explain this incident concerned him and he felt he needed to address my anger problem. He explained that this behaviour was improper and I needed to deal with this immediately. I responded to his rebuke and ended up dealing with my anger around this business meeting. I was thankful that he felt comfortable enough to challenge me.

Unfortunately, the relationship did not remain in this mentoring/friendship form. He was later asked to leave the church, which changed our relationship. He went to pastor a church on Vancouver Island, which changed our relationship. He was asked to leave that church, which changed our relationship. He came back to Merritt and formed a home church, which my family and I began to attend, which once again changed our relationship. My wife and I then left the home church and that dramatically changed our relationship. With that final departure, came the foundation of what I now call Experiential Authority.

Whenever one person has Positional Authority over another person, the propensity to take advantage of that power exists in that relationship. We can begin to recognize when this happens because the person with the Positional Authority begins to remove worth and value from the Listener through their words and actions. In the case of my relationship to this pastor, my worth and value became defined by him and conformity to his ideals became the entrance fee to his heart. When change and conformity becomes the hoops that we need to jump through in order to seek out acceptance and affirmation we can be aware that these actions are harmful and will continue to be harmful. If we find that it is happening to us, we can learn the use of boundaries in an effort to minimize the harm.

Boundaries were something new for me, and certainly a skill that I needed much help with. In fact, my understanding that such a concept existed did not come until a few years after my wife and I left the home church. Up until then, the idea of boundaries was instead some unhelpful ideas around intimate community and the related ideas of caring for one another. As I reflected on my various relationships with the pastor's family, I realized that I did not have healthy boundaries with any of them. Over the course of our time in that home church, I had hired both of the pastor's children, his brother-in-law, and I sold some of the products that his wife produced, all through the businesses that I was managing. I had felt the pressure and even responsibility to use my position in which to care for the pastor's family by providing employment opportunities for them.

The pressure to do this came out of the intimate community that was this home church and the idea that in some weird way it was our responsibility to care for the pastor and his family. By fulfilling my responsibility to care for the pastor and his family, I had along the line somewhere lost my ability to manage those family members who I hired. Whenever I had some work related concerns with his children, I was the one at fault, and it was my attitude that was getting in the way of 'true relationship and fellowship'. This was the beginning of language confusion. Whenever either my wife or I began to question the role and purpose of the home church, we were met with stern and corrective words. Language became quite a confusing construct of my relationship to the pastor and indeed to the home church. After a while, my wife and I were not sure what we thought.

An illustration of this language confusion was Jasmine's and my conviction to offer tithes to the place of worship that we attended. Out of a conviction, we began to give our tithes to the home church. In turn, the pastor, when Jasmine and I would confront him on the legitimacy of the home church, would tell us that because he had individuals tithing to the home church that made it legitimate. Thus, this type of circular logic and entwined language became quite confusing to the both of us. What I am referring to is rhetorical tautology. Rhetorical tautology is a constructed argument presented in such a way that the truth cannot be disputed. The argument self-references, thus making it unfalsifiable. It simply cannot be wrong because of how the language has been constructed. An example of rhetorical tautology would be because we tithed to the home church that made it a home church and because it was a home church, we tithed to it.

This home church became our entire world. We would meet in one form or another several times throughout the week, and slowly both my wife and I were pulling away from my family and hers. We were taught about the need to forsake family for the sake of intimacy in this church community. This became especially strong during the times that family were trying to challenge this home church. Consequently, both Jasmine and I became quite disconnected from our own families and we instead sought intimacy and family connection within the home church.

Since our individual worth and value was being defined by the pastor, every time we responded to new definitions of language in a positive way, we found affirmation and acceptance. Spurred on by this affirmation and acceptance, we continued to act in obedience to what was being taught, continuing not to listen or to seek language in order to describe our own emotional experiences. In retrospect, we can identify where repeatedly both my wife and I disregarded our own experiences and wisdom and took on the External Identities presented to us through this pastor and his teachings. I now describe this home church as an evangelical cult. Such was the extent of the pastor's Experiential Authority that we daily took our marching orders from him. The pastor defined our relationship with friends and even with each other. What we did and how we did it came from him and consequently our sense of worth and value was defined through him.

Our every experience needed to be affirmed through the pastor. As a result, we continued to deny our own stories, supressing our emotional language as well. In exchange, we would offer up obedient cognitive responses to these new External Identities that we were putting on. This was how the relationship had changed. From something helpful, where my marriage benefited because of that mentoring/friendship, to a place where my wife and I were suspicious of each other and we lived our marriage through the pastor.

Even though my relationship had changed to the pastor because of his leaving one church and then another and now being in this home church, the pastor was convinced that it had not. When I would desire to explore how our relationship had changed, he would often refer back to that coffee in the restaurant where I had made the decision to make myself accountable to him. Within that context, he would explain that this was what God was doing in the present and as a result, nothing had changed. This pastor was firm in describing me and defining our relationship with that one event in the restaurant. It did not matter how many years had passed or how much our lives were different now. It was not even a concern that our various roles and responsibilities had changed. In the end, I was still being defined as that young man who made himself accountable to his pastor.

There was no space in my relationship to the pastor in the present to explore how our relationship had changed in the past. Instead, whenever I would venture to talk about how our relationship had changed he would define me as rebellious. His description of me would be shared with my wife, my friends, and with the pastors that would come along in the new church that my wife and I were now attending. I simply could not escape from his descriptions of who he thought I was.

It took my wife and I several years to be able to process all the harm that had occurred during our time in this home church. In fact, for the year after we first left the home church we chose not to speak about the experience at all. There was a danger in us speaking about it because the words that we had learned how to use were not ours but the pastors', and we would end up hurting one another when we used them. We needed to seek out who we were individually, and relearn how to relate to one another safely, before we could begin to talk about our experience being in this home church.

This was a slow process and a careful one, where my wife and I would take much time and effort asking each other for clarification around what the other was saying. We were practising reflective listening skills in order to understand the various meanings we were assigning to our words. Ironically, we were using similar words with each other but with very different meanings. This meant taking more time in order to open up the space with each other to listen and explore language safely. Throughout this process, we also focused on listening to our emotions, which within the home church was all but dismissed, unless the pastor was expressing an emotion. In those instances, we were invited to participate emotionally, keeping it in check with the rest of the group. Now, from the safety of each other, my wife and I would give each other the space to express emotion, all initially without understanding.

In the silence of those moments, we waited upon the other to find the language that they wanted to use in order to describe their emotion. It was very freeing to have the space to explore our emotions, to name them, and to begin to think about the meaning behind much of the language that the pastor had used. At the end of this process, we had compiled a list of words and phrases that within the intimacy of the home church took on one meaning, yet prior to going to the home church and now after we had left, had completely different meanings. What we had found was a language embedded within a language. It would take me a few more years before I could explain what this idea around a language being embedded within a language meant.

The time did come when I could explain what this idea of embedded language was. It was now several years later, when sitting in a Seminary classroom learning about adolescent development, the phrase Experiential Authority came to my mind as the descriptor for that new language. I was troubled by what the professor was doing. He taught with authority and was a worldwide-recognized leader in youth and youth development. His communication style and presence in the room felt like we were with a star.

As he would speak about youth development concepts, I observed many of the students deciding to openly disregard their own experiences, especially in relation to their own children, and instead take on the experiences being presented by the professor. I struggled with what I was hearing. I could not fathom in one particular example how a parent of two teenagers could suddenly tell the professor that they finally understand their own children because of what the professor just said. This fellow classmate had completely minimized their own experience of raising their teenage children and had taken on the External Identity being presented by the instructor.

Up to this point, this type of encounter had remained largely an unlanguaged emotional experience. I was aware of how angry I was with what had just happened but could not find the language to express my emotional experience. When I was discussing my frustrations and emotions with a colleague and my wife, who was taking the course with me, I found the words Experiential Authority as a great fit to explain my emotional response. I began to work with those words, unpack them, and use them to discuss my own feelings of grossness and yucky-ness. Over the duration of this professor's course, I found that these descriptions of my experience and ultimately the language of Experiential Authority fit remarkably well.

I am troubled by the harm that Experiential Authority can do in people's lives because of what it does to the Listener's own sense of worth and value. It has taken me almost twenty years to find the language of Experiential Authority in order to describe those feelings of grossness and yucky-ness that I would feel when walking away from a conversation. Twenty years of encounters with individuals who, through their use of Positional Authority, would invite me to take their experience and make it my own.

Back when my wife and I were leaving the home church, I concluded that my focus should not be on trying to change the pastor. Instead, I needed to help myself recognize the harm caused by the pastor's use of Experiential Authority and ultimately seek out language to describe my emotional experience. I understand that once I could give voice to my emotional experience, the power and control that the pastor was imposing upon me could be broken. However, through this process, I needed to learn that instead of focusing on trying to reason with the person using Experiential Authority I had to only focus on minimizing the harm that it brought into my life. In my case, it took a couple of years communicating back and forth with this pastor and his wife, pointlessly trying to have them 'see' our point-of-view when the point of not changing the person became clear.

The final understanding of this idea of not trying to change the Speaker came when my wife and I were meeting the pastor and his wife one last time in order to seek reconciliation. During the course of that conversation, the subject of playing the board game Scrabble came up. The pastor was a prolific writer, spending hours each day to journal, write sermons, and teaching material, which made his response to my question quite profound and absurd. He mentioned to me that he did not play Scrabble because in his opinion it was a waste of words. 'A waste of words'. That phrase just hung in the air and in that moment, the fragmentation of our relationship seemed to make sense. I suddenly understood how meaningless it would be to try to make him understand the harm he had caused both my wife and I.

It became obvious that he did not want a relationship with me, or with anyone, because for this pastor, to have a relationship with someone was pointless. Instead he wanted 'mutual submission to one another' and to relate to one another as a 'brother in Christ'. This language was simply a mask for his External Identity designed for his followers, and defined by his Positional Authority from being my pastor. Consequently, there remained an invitation in that final conversation to dismiss my experience and replace it with his. The result would have me seeking a worth and value defined through him and often based in his own sense of right and wrong. The result from this type of interaction was harm, which had been my experience of him over the previous few years. In the end, the conclusion was that to play that game of Scrabble with him would end up simply being a waste of words.

Chapter 5 Language and Emotions

Language, shared within smaller, intimate communities contain meaning within larger meaning. This is what I call embedded language. Embedded language within a meta-language structure provides affirmation, intimacy, and connection to the individuals within these communities. The words may look the same in our dictionaries but their meanings are constructed within these communities and form the individualized lexicon of the participants. This type of shared communication reinforces messages of affirmation and acceptance within these smaller, intimate communities.

Having become a Christian a few years before I attended the church that the pastor of the home church first was, I had already become familiar with what I call Christianeze. Christianeze is the language associated with the Christian faith, often a series of words that imply a much more involved conversation. As an example, a Christian may say that they are 'justified' or 'justified through faith'. However, to a non-Christian, the complexity of this word is limited to their own experience of it, which may be far different then how it is understood within the Christian community. Therefore, complex topics within an intimate community can be shared using succinct words that may have multiple meanings outside of that community context.

A mutual intimacy within a smaller

community also reinforces this idea of language embedded within language. As individuals align themselves with these intimate communities, they seek out common language in which to gain affirmation and acceptance within the group. Many clubs, teams, and organizations have this embedded language as familiar vocabulary, largely unknown by someone on the outside. In a sense, this is a unique organizational behavior of these communities. By creating an embedded language, they have differentiated themselves from outsiders, thus reinforcing intimacy and connection within their own community.

In one instance, my wife and I were having breakfast in a restaurant connected to the hotel we were staying at. It was quiet on this particular morning as we sat there waiting for our breakfast to arrive. Across the room, two men were seated, finishing their breakfast. They were talking among themselves, loud enough that my wife and I could hear their conversation. The thing was, however, although we could hear their conversation we could not understand anything they were saying. We heard different words being spoken, and they were English words, but it was obvious that these men were speaking in a lingo associated to their work. The result was that these men understood each other and were connected to one another because of that understanding. However, my wife and I were unable to gain access to what was being said because of their use of language.

It was the use of this type of embedded

language, which contributed to making the home church being so difficult to walk away from. The confusing, yet intimate, and familiar use of language that the pastor used, caused me to seek meaning to a vocabulary I thought I already understood. In the moments of connection within this home church, the language was familiar, inviting, and easy to use. It came with a level of intimacy and it came with acceptance. I could speak, and was willing to speak, the language associated with the group. Therefore, through my use of this vocabulary, I was not only accepted but I received entwined messages of worth and value.

I had brought with me a familiar lexicon that was associated with Evangelical Christian circles, yet within this smaller home church environment the pastor began to change the meaning of those words. At first, this process felt like a time of discovery, and because I was enthusiastically responding to these new descriptions of familiar words, I was affirmed with messages of worth and value. It felt like I was becoming more knowledgeable of God's Word and that I had a deeper understanding of the various complexities surrounding Christian theology. Over time, I learned new meanings to old words. Consciously, I made the decision to dismiss old meanings in order to embrace the new vocabulary of this home church.

Unknown to me at the time, what was happening was I was continuing to take on the External Identities that the pastor was imposing. I longed for connection, and for intimacy, and without knowing it, my worth and value was now being defined through my obedience to this pastor. The appeal of this External Identity was that it seemed to come without any pain. The packaging was wrapped around old familiar language of 'freedom in Christ'. This was something I sought after enthusiastically, as my experiences had much pain, hurt, and anguish woven throughout. The appeal to find and embrace an experience that seemed to be free from such hard emotions grew more and more appealing to me.

However, what I did not realize at the time was the ultimate cost that such a process would bring. In the process of learning and embracing this new language, seeking affirmation and connection, I disregarded my own experiences and fully embraced a new identity presented by the pastor. Ultimately, I ended up muffling my own voice and associated messages of worth and value, embracing instead the definitions of worth and value that came from the pastor. The result was that the pastor defined who I was through his own presuppositions and his own experiential knowledge. My new experiences in this environment were filtered through his understanding and his teaching. Consequently, the pastor, using the language associated with this intimate community, defined my own understanding of my experiences.

Because I had taken on his External Identity, my own sense of worth and value needed to come through what he was saying.

Thus, when, out of my own experiences, I sought to find my own voice, and find my own language for my emotions, I was labelled as being rebellious. In this sense, even the meaning of the word rebellious had changed, with rebelliousness now resembling disobedience to the pastor, although I was not able to see it that clearly while a part of the home church. The pastor rewrote the old language associated with Christian fellowship. Christian fellowship meant an intimate community of like-minded believers, and an invitation and affirmation of being some place where you are welcome and belong. However, a key characteristic in the rewriting of this old language was that the pastor rewrote it to come with a set of rules and behavioral expectations.

If I wanted fellowship then I needed to first understand and accept the pastor's new definition of that word. This process of seeking fellowship was followed by having to change my experience and my past behaviors associated with that word. I had to silence my voice in order to hear and obey this new language. This controlling structure using language combined with a set of rules and behavioral expectations is found in historic psychology. Historic psychology used probing questions such as, "What's under that?" in order to probe past all of the 'surface' issues that the *patient* brought to each session. "What's under that?" came with an embedded behavioral expectation. The rule was that the patient needed to keep revealing things until the psychologist was convinced that they had found the underlying cause.

It seems like many of today's church communities are still relying on this old methodology in order to construct new meaning to language. An example of this is someone seeking to understand his or her relationship to God. The pastor and others within this intimate community may have behavioral expectations for the person seeking affirmation in their relationship to God. Until that person finds the correct language and the correct behaviors, they are deemed not quite right in their relationship to God. This, then, becomes the behavioral rule imposed upon the congregant. If the person truly desires affirmation and intimacy within this community, they would be expected to adjust their behaviors and seek the correct language to support their behaviors.

Thus, I believe that my home church experience is not uncommon, but is shared by many others. The summary of this experience is this idea that the Speaker, in a place of authority within this intimate community, will use the language shared by everyone within this community, in order to gain manipulative control over the Listener. The Speaker then defines the Listener's experience using commonly shared language native to this intimate community. Subsequently, because the Listener has not been given the space to explore language in order to explain their experience, they are forced to take on this External Identity by the Speaker. However, in taking on this External Identity from the Speaker, the Listener is taking on an experience, which has these embedded behavioral expectations included with them. The Speaker has used their position within this intimate community in which to define the Listener's experience.

Therefore, all messages related to worth and value will end up being defined through the Speaker to the Listener because of the External Identity that the Listener has taken on. The Listener has identified both the language and experience of the Speaker as representing a correct behavior within this intimate community. As a result, the Listener will then seek to emulate those correct behaviors in order to gain acceptance and affirmation of this intimate community. The Listener will not gain acceptance and affirmation until they adjust their behaviors and utilize the associated language emulated by this intimate community.

At the end of our time attending the home church, my wife and I were using the same familiar language associated with Evangelical Christian community, yet so much of it took on very different meanings. When we had left the home church and were reconnecting to the greater church community, the embedded language we had learned isolated us from them. The word 'program' had very negative connotations as an example. Within the home church, if another church was putting on a new program, they were seen as doing church 'man's way' and not God's way. Consequently, even though there was lots of similar type activities that the home church was doing, which could be described as 'programs', it was instead referred to as following God's activity and 'joining God in His work'.

Looking back, I have a larger perspective on how we ended up attending a home church that had a pastor who exerted Experiential Authority in such harmful ways. When I first met this pastor, I was carrying a lot of hurts and pains. My wife and I began a relationship with this pastor as a young married couple just starting a family. I found much affirmation and acceptance from the pastor and that was soothing to me. I was looking for an experience that was relatively pain free yet still had embedded in it strong messages of worth and value.

As I began to form a strong relationship to this pastor, my hurts and pains were diminishing, as I took on the External Identity that he was offering. I sought affirmation and acceptance through him because of the associated embedded messages of worth and value. In order to do that I changed my language to emulate what he was saying. Over time, our relationship had changed but the space for me to explore how those changes had affected me was not there. In my attempt to explore my emotional experiences, I was labelled as rebellious. This label was an attack against the affirmation and acceptance that I had previously enjoyed and so it created internal conflict. In the end, my emotional experiences sought their own voice and in order to give myself the space needed to explore that voice I needed to say no to the pastor's voice.

The hardest part of removing these External Identities was to find my own voice and say no. The hardest part of saying no was to say it from a place of social isolation. I had left the home church but because of the language learned in the home church, I was without a compatible vocabulary within the larger church community. To say no, meant to disregard the External Identities that this pastor had been giving to me and to take up my own painful experiences once again. Somehow, I needed to be okay with my own pain and loss and to find my own language to describe those experiences. The first step, then, was to say no to the External Identities and yes to the pain and loss.

The shedding of these External Identities also meant the disconnecting from the attached messages of worth and value. This meant that I had to begin an equally hard journey of discovering my own intrinsic worth and value that went beyond anyone's description of such. This was very difficult because of the use of language within the home church to ascribe meaning to my experiences. It was as if I needed to be comfortable with sitting in my own muck long enough to describe the emotions I felt around those painful experiences. I had sought freedom from my own pain and loss, and in the seeking of that freedom, I took up the descriptions of my worth and value defined through the pastor of this home church. Now, in order to find that freedom I was initially looking for, I needed to first understand my worth and value from this place of pain and loss. This meant being okay in my brokenness, and the associated vulnerability that came with sharing it.

The reality was that I had gone along in life degrading my emotional capacity to some subservient place within, where it found no voice to share its experiences. In times of pain and loss, I simply disconnected from the experience and associated emotions. This coping mechanism had served me well in order to survive some hard times but now it was time to discover that I had an intrinsic worth and value that was beyond any pastor's, or any one's ability to measure it. I had to discover that along with my pain and loss, I had a worth and value that was beyond measure. To find the freedom from my pain and loss that I was looking for, I had to acknowledge the equality of my emotional capacity and sit long enough in my own muck to give that capacity a voice.

This journey continues to this day and continues to be painful at times. Sometimes I need to walk out of the room when a show or movie becomes too emotional for me and I feel overwhelmed with my emotion. At times, I am aware that my emotional reaction is too much in relation to the content I am watching. At these moments, I seek a safe place to be able to express, most often without words, the pain that I am feeling. I have much muck to sit in and I do so slowly and sensitively, knowing how easily overwhelmed I can become when experiencing emotion. This comes from spending much of my life dissociated from most emotion, seeking power and control in which to supress it. Language, therefore, becomes an important tool in understanding our emotion.

Language is the power we give to an experience. Language is the vehicle in which we use to share that experience with one another. In the process of seeking language for our emotions, in an effort to give voice to and understand our emotional experiences, we must become comfortable with the fragmented nature of the process. We may find a word that we have associated to a particular emotion or emotional experience, which no longer fits. In this moment, we need to be okay with discarding that word and trying another one on. We must also learn to be comfortable with the fragmented process that finding language for emotions can bring. Languaged emotions will not unfold in a linear, chronological fashion, bringing a cognitive understanding to the experience. More often than not, languaged emotions are scattered, fragmented, and disorientating.

In a therapeutic setting, the client may seem to be feeling two ways about something. This ambiguous emotional state can be frustrating but counselors and therapists recognize the value in being in such a place. During these moments, the therapists will pay particular attention to the words used and work hard to use reflective listening skills in order to hear accurately what it is that the client is saying. Emotions allow for a coexisting state of being. Emotions are comfortable with ambiguity as this gives the maximum amount of space needed in order to explore different language around these emotional experiences. Therefore, language becomes a helpful tool in the exploration of our emotional experiences.

Woven into our languaged emotional experiences is a disproportionate use of cognitive communication versus emotive communication. Emotion-laded communication ends up being relegated to a subservient role in both communication and function. It would seem that there is not much use for emotion in communication. Emotion tends to get in the way of communicating and is used only as a theatrical prop, a cue to the listener about what is going to be heard next. Thus, the space and language to explore our emotional experiences becomes quite limited and we feel the pressure to 'think' our emotions, rather than to 'feel' them.

Today, the only place emotion is given any sense of equality is among the Arts. However, even in Arts, the cognitive descriptions of the Arts tend to dismiss these emotional expressions. When there is an emotional expression, there tends to be a well thought out formulaic equation to what needs to be expressed as an emotion and at what point in the presentation. Therefore, there exists a limited range of emotion-laded vocabulary and the related space to have those emotions expressed within such academic structures.

What we have done as a society then is to relegate our emotional expressions to a subservient place. This was done through the containment of the people's emotional expressions coming out of the Renaissance Period, mixed with the modernistic structures around knowledge. What became clear to the rationalists during this period was that emotions could not be trusted. Consequently, what could not be trusted should not be expressed, and what could not be expressed should not have any sort of place at the learned table of understanding.

How much we have lost as a society after leaving the importance of emotion behind with the Renaissance, bringing about the Age of Reason, Scientific Thought, and Rational Belief. Society has devalued the worth of emotion over reason. In their quest for objective knowledge, the rationalists reasoned away emotion, believing it to hinder that journey, seeing it as a flaw of humankind perhaps. Today, emotion finds outlets in the fringes of society, in religious extremism, in radical groups chasing all types of causes, and in Arts. Today, emotions continue to be demeaned and devalued, instead of being used to give us cues or ideas around whom we might be, who we want to be, and who we are being forced to be.

It is these old ideas that relegate an emotional woman to a description of neuroses, dating back to 1896, when Sigmund Freud published *The Aetiology of Hysteria*. These old ideas rationalize the broken and fragmented emotional words into a structured 'deeper meaning', relying on over one hundred year-old psychoanalytical methodology to help make sense of this nonsense. These old ideas continue, perpetuating stereotypes, reinforcing racism, and isolating the unknown. This happens because emotional words cannot be understood, in light of the lack of space given to explore them and ultimately to find language for them.

Emotions and emotional expressions are treated like a scientific discovery during the dark ages. We do not take the time to explore language in order to add voice to our emotions. We do not seek to understand our emotions; instead, we are simply bothered that they are there in the first place. Nevertheless, they do not go away and in an incredible way, our emotions seek out equality with our cognitive expressions in many different forms. From a psychological point-of-view, our unspoken emotions tend to disrupt our various relationships and systems that we are a part of in order to find a voice. They intrude our dreams and biologically they form their own specialized memories if not connected to our cognitive sides.

In every way if our emotions cannot find an equal voice against the tyranny of cognitive expression then it will seek it out. Sometimes such non-verbal or fragmented verbalized emotions tend to overwhelm the person expressing them. This expression of our emotions can be seen or experienced as chaotic, broken, out of control, or disruptive. However, our emotions are meant to be felt as much as our cognitions are meant to be thought. We seek to control, supress, deny, and minimize these emotions because there is not the space to understand them. We need to understand that the denial of space does not help us achieve the goal of controlling our emotions or supressing them, instead it simply prolongs the inevitable expression of them.

This emotional experience is made even more complicated when we feel something but struggle to find the language to describe what it is that we feel. Oddly enough, to deny, minimize, or even supress an emotion we need to be aware of what it is that we are feeling. However, when the emotion has not yet found language to describe it, and we attempt to push it away, the emotion will return, seeking the language to describe itself. This cyclical nature of unlanguaged emotion will continue to escalate until it finds voice and space to be expressive. During this process, our lives may become greatly disrupted, turning to confusion and disconnectedness.

In early childhood development, we can see this illustrated with the child who is learning language and during the process of trying to verbalize their emotion their meanings becomes frustrated and agitated. They are aware of what they are feeling but when trying to express it through verbal communication they may not have found a word that clearly communicates what they are feeling. The result is a layered expression of emotion, which speaking from the experience of being a parent, becomes a frustrating experience for both the child and the caregiver. As hard as this process of verbalizing emotional language is, the whole process is further complicated when trauma or loss is experienced. In the experience of trauma or loss, our emotions become more prominent and perhaps even overwhelming. Without the language or space to express what those emotions are, we may end up disconnecting from them in an effort to survive and move on.

It is not that the emotions felt have left but instead, in an effort to care for oneself, the unlanguaged emotions were disconnected from. This disconnect does not remove the emotion but merely leaves it separate from its cognitive counterpart, which renders the impact of the felt emotion neutral for a time. Part of the healing journey, therefore, will mean addressing this unlanguaged emotion, feeling it, and naming it. This amazing process is a result of how our memory works. We experience our environment through our sensory organs, our emotional capacities, and our cognitive capacities all separately. Our mind then takes all of this data input and weaves it together with a sort of internal timestamp to help us re-experience the memory when recalled later. When recalled, sensory data stored in different parts of the brain are reconstructed in the 'remembering' process, based on the associated timestamp.

An example of this remembering process is one's first kiss or a special encounter with an older family member, such as a grandparent. During the remembering process the reconstructed memory would be described with words describing the scene, words describing the sensory input (sights, sounds, smells), along with words describing the associated feelings. Our recall of the particular memory is presented this way, often with all three elements included and if possible, woven together into such a description as to help the listener imagine that they are there as well.

However, in examples where there is a disconnection from the emotional experience of a memory, such as trauma or loss, the memory recall may appear fragmented, or broken. This is because the brain has stored some of the details with a timestamp but not all of the information. In this example, it would be possible to recall a traumatic event without any expression of emotion, simply because the person has disconnected from it. During the recall of that traumatic event, their brains did not recall the emotions since they did not have the associated timestamp.

In more severe cases, where obvious dissociation has occurred, there are specialized techniques that should be used. These techniques help the person find language for the unlanguaged emotions that are being felt but are noticeably disconnected to any sense of internal timestamp. The challenge in these types of situations is to be aware of our presuppositions and our own stories of loss, as a beginning point in conversation, since so much harm can come to the person we are listening to if we are not careful. Such techniques are discussed in my work with a type of therapy I have developed, called

Narrative Memory Therapy; however, I will touch on some summary thoughts here.

Finding the language to describe our emotional experiences is a very important part in the process of equalizing our emotional capacities with our cognitive capacities. Our cognition is most often the accumulation of rational learning, a reflection of our environment, our community, and our culture. We learn the answers and we learn the reasons for everything around us through these reflections. However, our emotion helps enrich each of these reflections, reinforcing the cognitive summaries through experiential learning. During this process of experiential learning, we explore vocabulary to find the language to represent our emotion. By learning to listen to our emotional responses, and then find the language to name them, they will then serve as a support to the cognitive explanation of our experiential learning. This relationship between our cognitive processes and our emotive processes becomes equal with each fulfilling their unique roles.

A breakdown of this process occurs when one's emotional experience falls outside of their rational understanding. This is the case with trauma or severe loss. In severe cases, the cognitive recall of trauma or severe loss will become independent from one's emotional experience of the event. This will leave their rational understanding as the only immediately accessible recall of the event. During this process, disconnect occurs or what I refer to as a fragmentation. In most cases, the emotional experience does not have language to describe itself and it becomes fragmented off in order for the person to continue to function. When the experience is recalled later, the person only has a strictly cognitive recall of it or a non-verbal emotive recall. In more severe cases, there is no recall at all.

A non-verbal emotive recall could also be referred to as a somatic memory or 'body' memory. A somatic memory can be observed through body language that the person is 'remembering' or experiencing something but may not be able to find the language to describe what that is. Among other ways, this is observed through the clenching of fists, the rocking back and forth of the body, or the person's description of self. An example might be "I feel really cold right now", or "my heart is racing and I don't know why". Instead of the need to understand and rationalize why we may be clenching our fists or 'feeling really cold', which would be the 'thought' reaction to what is going on, we can instead focus on naming the feeling.

It is important to not focus on the 'why' aspect, such as why we may be clenching our fists, but instead on the 'what', as in what are we feeling when we clench our fists. In this sense, because our presupposition is that all emotions are logical, it becomes okay to state that we are 'feeling really cold' right now, without needing to accompany that feeling with some cognitive understanding. Our assumption is merely that we are cold and that is logical even though we may not necessarily understand why immediately. We are elevating the 'fact' that we are cold to an equal place beside our cognitive reasoning when we acknowledge that our emotional feeling is logical, even though there is no immediate, rational understanding.

Within the space of unlanguaged emotion is where Experiential Authority is the most harmful. This is because the Speaker using Experiential Authority is presenting an experience to the Listener, inviting the Listener to take on the Speaker's experience at the expense of the Listener's own experience. The Listener may disregard their own fragmented experiences, seeking to find some normality or some sense of what is going on in light of their own anxiety. This fear then motivates the Listener to embrace the experience of the Speaker, in hopes that what is presented will bring some sense of meaning to their own fragmentation. Unfortunately, because the Listener has taken the experience being presented by the Speaker, they have also taken the Speaker's description of worth and value. The Speaker's description of worth and value then masks the Listener's own unlanguaged emotional experiences, limiting the space to explore those damaged nerve-endings.

The result is that the Listener now finds his or her own sense of worth and value only through the Speaker. This gives the Speaker an incredible amount of power over the Listener. It invites the Speaker to offer an external sense of identity to the Listener.

Throughout this process, the Listener's own emotions are not being listened to. However, the amazing thing about our emotions is that they will find a way to be heard. Because the emotions may not have yet found the verbal language to express themselves, this process may look messy, disorientating, and disruptive. What is needed is both the time and the space to sit in that muck and to listen to the unlanguaged emotion until the Listener can find language to describe it.

This process of listening to our emotional language is made more complicated given that the Speaker's External Identity comes with language that contains meaning for the Speaker. When the Listener takes on that identity, they also take on the associated language of that identity. The Listener then seeks to integrate those words with the associated meaning as their own. When the Listener seeks to find language for their own emotions, often the words they seek may clash with the ones already imposed upon them. The word may be the same but it will have two completely different meanings. The process of differentiating from the Speakers' associated language and the Listener's own discovery of language for their own emotional experiences is what I describe as being like a caterpillar going through metamorphosis. It is often violent and chaotic as the Listener pushes against the constraints of the Speaker's language in order to emerge with their own language.

As disruptive as this process may be, the Listener will need to take all the time and space that they require in which to explore their emotional experiences. As they acknowledge that they first do have unlanguaged emotional experiences, they can then seek out language to describe those emotional experiences. The Listener has given voice to these emotions and in so doing has spoken against the External Identity from the Speaker. Within this process, the Listener has treated their emotional capacity as equal to their cognitive capacity. This exploration of emotions, in order to name them through verbalized language, becomes both freeing and empowering to the Listener, who has spoken against the External Identity from the Speaker.

Chapter 6 Emotional Capacity vs Cognitive Capacity

As I sought to describe the journey of someone seeking language to match his or her emotional experiences, I turned to a great author, Bréne Brown. She introduced the language of vulnerability and I was intrigued with how well it fit. Her description of vulnerability turns fear on its head and reveals a strength, which sets a person free. She has spent several years studying shame and those journeys lead her to explore vulnerability and its positive uses in combating fear. Vulnerability became the bridge between one's unspoken emotional experiences and one's cognitive experiences. I was genuinely excited by her work.

Nevertheless, society continues to perpetuate a divide between the emotional capacity, vulnerability, of a person and the intellectual capacity, or cognitive abilities of a person. Society, culture, and structured communities tend to frame the rules of each of these capacities by limiting and defining how both are used, at, and in, any given moment. I continue to advocate for an acknowledgment that both our emotional and our cognitive selves are to be treated and respected as equals, both defining the other, and only limited by our inability to find the language to define either.

However, within the Evangelical community it would seem that there is a different sort of system at work when interacting with either of these capacities. This tends to mess things up quite a lot, when trying to understand the harmful aspects of Experiential Authority, as it exists within the Church. This is because the harmful use of power, as exhibited through Experiential Authority, tends to be presented in a particular way. In a church where the cognitive capacity is seen and appreciated as the dominant trait of a person, my observation is that Experiential Authority is, or tends to be, presented through emotional outlets. In a church where the emotional capacity is seen and appreciated as the dominant trait, my observation is that Experiential Authority is presented through cognitive outlets. What I conclude from my observations is that there is a way to use Experiential Authority in a manner that will manipulate and control a person or a group of people.

An example might be in a conservative church where classic hymns are sung all in the same key, and limited, in order to make way for longer sermons full of Scripture references about what we should be doing. In this particular example, when an active participant of this church begins to speak with Experiential Authority it is most notably accentuated using emotional words. This contrast seems to help elevate the importance of the person speaking, almost without objection. In a charismatic church, much emotion is found in their prominent expression of worship and even in the emotional punch of their sermons. When an active participant of this church begins to speak with Experiential Authority, it tends to be accentuated using emotionless words with an emphasis on the cognitive value of insight and reason. Again, it would seem that this contrast seems to help elevate the Speaker without objection.

This contextual contrast tends to set the stage for the Speaker using Experiential Authority. Because the people are in what should normally be an intimate and mutually beneficial environment, it would seem that the situation is perfect for a misuse of power and authority. 'Thus sayeth the Lord', tends to function like a golden ticket in this environment, as it already is speaking to the Listener's own desires to connect with God in an intimate way. It is that insecurity which is preyed upon, or exploited, and I am rather troubled with.

Without an appreciation of relational dynamics and/or power differentials that may be present in any conversation, the natural place of authority for the Speaker within a group of people can easily become harmful. That is how easy it would be for someone who is not aware. How much more harmful it is when someone is aware, and they press on with a desire to be known and recognized as one with authority within this group of people. Because of the intimacy of the environment in which everyone is participating, it would be easy to use Experiential Authority to sway and leverage control over the group of people.

All the Speaker needs to do is to accentuate the opposite of the norm, whether it is emotive or cognitive-based, and finish off with an "in Jesus name" and the process is validated, accepted, and given authority. In this way, the Speaker defines truth and objective knowledge, and through it all, the Listener's own worth and value becomes defined by the Speaker. One can therefore begin to appreciate the magnitude of harm that occurs when someone within the church begins to operate with Experiential Authority. "In Jesus name" is sounding a lot more like a bullet with our name on it.

The corrective in the midst of this harmful environment is to treat both our cognitive and emotive capacities as equal. When one capacity is used or valued over the other, we should be aware that the potential for a misuse of power is present. So how do we weigh both capacities as equal? Do we simply learn how to listen to our emotions? How do we listen to our emotions? Is this a cognitive function? Do we then utilize our cognitive capacity in order to listen to our emotive capacity?

Actually, the cognitive capacity to listen to emotions is an oxymoron. It hears but I do not believe that it listens. To listen is to invite perspective, collaboration, and community, and yes, emotion, into the conversation. Cognition hears and reasons. Like an industrial machine, cognition logically applies modern principles of intelligence, reasoning, morality, and scientific thought to all that it hears, and through that process, like a juicer, all emotion is squeezed out.

The dilemma in this process of

listening to our emotions comes when within the intimate community, the argument presented is that the cognitive capacity is listened to and reasoned with the emotional expression. This is simply a fancy way of explaining how all emotion was squeezed out. It implies a hierarchical structure where cognition rules and emotion serves. I am frustrated just thinking about this and in particular how much these ideas have permeated the Evangelical Christian Church.

When I speak about Experiential Authority in the church, my descriptions of such could begin with the pastor, as that position is the most obvious. Still, it has been my own experience, and I suspect the experience of many others, that one does not need to be the pastor to use Experiential Authority within the local church. Within the walls of the Church, the very language of Christianity could easily become the pulpit from which Experiential Authority brings its harm to the people.

There is an idea woven into these ideas that not only touch on messages around worth and value but also expose a harmful viewpoint on the value of emotions. Our worth and value is not simply a cognitive function but an emotional one as well. When I unpack this idea further, I encounter the devaluing language of Experiential Authority. Upon examining it further, I find that there is an underlining presupposition surrounding our emotional capacities that further contributes to the harm it is causing. I can open up the space to have a dialogue about the importance of emotions and the value of listening to them and the conversation is reasoned away. It is countered with cognitive arguments talking about the over-emotional expression of emotions. How can such emotions have a place within the orderly structure of God's church?

Moreover, just in case you pop your head into one of those emotion-laded churches, the rational cognitive argument that is presented is about the self-control of the Spirit working through us. For that reason, as far as I can derive from these cognitive cogs, is that emotion needs to be self-controlled, contained, and collared, if it is going to be given any place within the Church. Folly is my response. I am not writing about just any folly, but folly that takes a foolish man and provides him with a place of honor, power, and authority. I am writing about a dangerous folly. This folly will harm, some out of its own ignorance, but some out of a place of thinking that they are right. This is the most dangerous folly of them all.

We search for both the space and the words to express our emotions but because they are emotions, they are not listened to. Instead, they are heard, and in hearing, our emotions are immediately sat in judgment of, rendering our defence useless. Such is the dilemma of the Church. Such is its folly. How can one approach the Cross, without emotion? How can one seek a forgiveness of sins without emotion? How can one come to know God without emotion? How twisted it is when our cognitive capacities clothe themselves with emotional garments long enough to get close to the cross. Emotions are not about reason as that completely misses the point. Emotions are about feelings and the exploratory journey that this takes us on.

Are we so concerned that our emotional capacities will lead us astray that we seek to restrain them before we begin? Why can't we cry out from the depths of ourselves, grasping at language to find form to our emotional expressions without the entire experience being rationalized away for lack of form and purpose? What is grief but a story without words? Is grief not accepted then because of its lack of form? That is the trouble, isn't it? This is the fear that I face – that grief and other wordless stories have no place in the Church because cognitive conformity forces itself upon us. We are invited to take on the External Identities of the foolish ones while we forsake our own worth and value in the process.

This talk about emotion is critical to the central tenants of Experiential Authority. This is critical because our emotions first alert us to the presence of Experiential Authority. It is also our emotions that help guide our response to Experiential Authority. I first describe Experiential Authority as this yucky, gross feeling that one gets inside them, that propels the Listener to a place of self-abasement in its most cruel intentions. These feelings have the Listener yielding to the power and experience of the Speaker, ultimately choosing to replace their personal experience and associated learning with what is presented to them as authoritative. This process ultimately seeks to create new learning environments where the Listener minimizes their own experiences and seeks to find affirmation and acceptance through the Speaker. Most of this happens at an emotional level and does not reveal itself until sometime after the event has occurred.

This may lead the Listener, who is feeling yucky and gross, to a place of self-blaming, guilt, shame, and a general feeling of inferiority. The Listener will struggle with these feelings, not sure of what they are feeling, perhaps, as the Speaker's External Identity begins to take root. Through this process, the Listener will seek out affirming messages of worth and value through the Speaker in an attempt to counteract their feelings of yucky-ness and grossness.

Subsequently, I can begin a lecture on Experiential Authority with the question, "Do you ever feel yucky or gross inside after talking with someone and you don't know why?", and I can receive many affirmative responses as they lean forward in their seats, hoping I can explain why that may be the case. In my explanation, I seek succinctness, but I find I must detract from my explanation of Experiential Authority in favor of a much more detailed explanation of our emotional self, versus our cognitive self. I would like to think that my detraction is not an effort to come across using Experiential Authority, (and this continues to be my motivator), for then I have accomplished nothing except to move the allegiance from one person of power to another.

Instead, I am compelled in my explanation of Experiential Authority to offer commentary on issues related to worth and value, gender equality, and the need to elevate emotive functions to the same place as our cognitive functions. The hope is that through this delineated process, the Listener will have gained a sense of empowerment. Through this empowerment, the Listener will have created enough space for them to measure whether or not what they experienced was Experiential Authority. This would then result in removing the Speaker, and the Speaker's explanation, as one more expert inviting the Listener to replace their experience with the Speaker's.

I mentioned gender equality as an important tangent in the explanation of Experiential Authority and so please allow me a moment to speak to this important aspect. When I have been in conversation and I am listening to the gender message woven into the language used, I hear an inequality between cognition and emotion. This has seemed to be the strongest when talking with men, in the sense that the gender message woven into the conversation is that cognition is of a higher value or a higher worth, than emotion.

I suppose I should be thankful that there is now at least some space in a male conversation to talk about emotions but it seems to be a rest stop on our way to 'true understanding'. This idea of stopping long enough, other than to change this flat tire of emotion, and give voice and description to the emotion, is not a popular idea at best, and at worst reveals a dominate societal message around gender stereotypes. The dominate societal message is that there is an inequality between the cognitive and the emotive male capacities. This societal message is that the male gender can experience feelings, but they need to 'understand' them in order to have the feeling process completed.

The implication is that although feelings are recognized, they are relegated to a place of lower importance and lower value over the place of cognitive, rational, thought. Added to this, it would seem that an emotional man is seen as having lower value and worth than those men who exert their cognitive capabilities. This clear inequality between the cognitive capacity and the emotional capacity shuts down the opportunity to give voice to the feelings, to understand them, and to find words to describe them. This inequality is ultimately a power-over stance that has a societal imposed definition attached to it. This definition is that emotional men have less value than cognitive men.

The descriptions we give to emotions and the casting out of our nets for words that fit the experience needs to be guarded and cherished for what it is. Therefore, we need to give it a place of equality with our cognitive selves. This process cannot look like a simple word exercise behind a thinly veiled attempt to 'understand' our emotions. Instead, it is a place of tension and ambiguity, where we can explore the vehicle of language to see what best fits with our emotion. Through the construction of language we show worth and value to our emotions and demonstrate its equality to our cognition. Such equality minimizes the power stance of the cognitive message and allows the voice of emotion to be heard.

Such messages of equality are powerful and healing – validating and affirming – to the one exploring language for their emotional experiences. When a male feels comfortable to share an exploratory emotion in conversation, our words should open up the space for that male to continue their descriptive construction of that emotion. This is done in order to validate their experience. Such language is difficult on one's own to try to construct, explore, and discover, and it saddens me that we make this process so much more difficult in conversation with men.

Often what we say is not what we mean. It is not enough to use words when we communicate because that would not be helpful. There is an old cliché that states, "Say what you mean and mean what you say". There needs to be an emphasis placed on the meaning behind our words, which would lead to an acknowledgement of understanding where they come from. Given society's constraints on emotional conversations for men, a lot of emotion is masked in cognitive constructed language. This will then misconstrue the meaning of the words being used by men. Each word has a dictionary definition and an etymology but in particular, with the English language, and I suspect this might be the case with other languages; it is *how* we say the word, which reveals the 'real' meaning of the word. It is our body language and the various intonations that we surround our words with that will inevitably create space or shut down space in any conversation.

When I think about these ideas from a gender-saturated point of view, there is a societal encoding that is present in most of our spoken language. Simply put, our spoken language has gender-specific meanings attached to it that may or may not have anything to do with the dictionary definition or etymology of the word. We use words to convey our message and our meaning behind the message. We use words to try to explain our emotions and to explain our experiences. The words we use are very personal and are chosen based on our experience and interaction with those words over the years that we have been exposed to them. These words are our words and in the use of them, we are creating the space for ourselves in order to find a fulfilling expression of all that we want to communicate.

If we were to use this same strategy or methodology when communicating with another, all that we will have been able to accomplish is to feel good about what we were able to communicate – our ideas, our experiences, and our feelings. The likelihood of creating any space for the person we are communicating with, to share their ideas, experiences, and feelings, would have been limited to our use and meaning of the words shared. Consequently, in using words to create space we must first learn how to listen to what the other is saying. In active listening, we must learn how to use the words of the person we are listening to, in the same way that they are using those words. As an example, reflective listening is a good skill to use in order to understand the effectiveness of listening and creating space.

With reflective listening the Listener summarizes bits of what the Speaker is saying, making sure to reflect back the same language in order to check in with the Speaker if they were listening correctly. In the summarization, the Listener uses the same words that the Speaker just used but presents it with the meaning that they think the Speaker is implying. Therefore, how much more important it is when a man and a woman are communicating with one another, because of the gender use and misuse of many of our spoken words. In order to create space in a conversation with a male, as an example, the female must learn to use the words presented by the male in the same way that the male has given them, because of the implied gender meaning behind many of these words. It works the other way as well, of course, which is why communication is still a very difficult thing to gain mastery over.

I will end this chapter with one

example of these ideas. If a man is talking to his partner, a female, and he wants to talk about the *intimacy* of their relationship, there is a gender meaning that is embedded into that word. However, the female may have a completely different understanding of what the word *intimacy* means than her male partner. In order to create space in the conversation, the female first seeks to understand what the male means when he says intimacy. She will then use the word intimacy in the same way as he has used it. In that process, space is opened up by their words and a healthier conversation can occur.

When the woman has established what her male partner means by the use of the word intimacy, in turn the male can seek to understand his female partner's use of the word intimacy. This process of listening to understand is never one-sided and remains active throughout the conversation. Equally, it is important to note that although I have been specific to a gender difference in the meaning assigned to words, even with same gender conversations there is a propensity to assign different meanings to the same words.

In order for healthy communication to occur, the participants in a conversation need to recognize that although cognition or reasoning have a place in that conversation, space must be created to explore both the emotional components of the words shared, along with the individualized meaning assigned to the words shared. This makes a conversation much more work but yields richness filled with mutual embedded messages of worth and value. To illustrate this point, think about arriving at a destination where several acquaintances are. A typical greeting may involve your acquaintance noticing you and saying, "Hey! How are you?" I wrote *say* over *ask* because this is not a question that is being asked but is simply a statement. The chances that this acquaintance is truly interested in the answer to the question, "How are you?" is quite slim. Why? Because it is emotionally-based and in a cognitive-saturated society, we simply do not have the time to include any emotional descriptions.

Such a greeting minimizes our emotional capacities and reinforces negative messages around worth and value. Such a greeting does more harm than good. It is time that we stopped using such 'greetings' and became more genuine in our exchanges with one another. Next time you greet someone with a "How are you?" pause long enough to hear their answer. If they get over being perplexed as to why you have waited for a response, perhaps a meaningful conversation can then occur. We have then helped in equalizing our emotional capacities against our cognitive capacities.

Chapter 7 Disconnection

The heat beat down on my back like the lashing of a whip. Waves rose in wisps of steam from the gravel road that lay before me. The lonely trees that were scattered among the countryside gasped for a breath of fresh air in the midst of this humidity. A light breeze began but even the blades of grass beneath the trees were too tired to respond. The only sign of water were the beads of perspiration rolling down my face.

I landed with a thud next to a rooted old tree, which offered only a few feet of shade. As I sat there catching my breath and patting my swollen lips with my sweat-soaked handkerchief a cold chill ran up my spine sending goose bumps down my arms. The parched leaves above me quivered in the wind. With a scream, a sharp, bitter cold gust of wind raced through the trees. As quickly as it started, it stopped, and in the stillness that followed a frozen snowflake landed on my nose melting on contact.

I looked up to see a sky obliterated by snowflakes. One by one, they landed on the ground melting as they made contact. With a shrill cry, the wind returned bringing an intensity of snowflakes reminiscent of a Yukon blizzard. I sat there shivering with my nose running, grasping my knees for warmth. All around me, the ground turned as white as a clean sheet falling onto a bed.

The branches above me started to sag under the weight of all the snow. The sky was turning a hazy white. I knew I would freeze if I stayed under this tree any longer. I got up, brushed the snow off and shook my head. As I blinked and opened my eyes there ahead of me were heat waves rising in wisps of steam from a parched gravel road heading off into the distance.

This was a story that I wrote about twenty years ago. I would sometimes come to a point in my life in which I needed to express myself in poetry, drawings, or in the writing of short stories. I found that I could protect my feelings through my mask of writing, embedding my disconnected emotions deep within the written lines, and in so provide me with a safe outlet for those feelings. The safety came through a sense of security, a safe built of words to protect the feelings from anyone who may want to threaten them or take them from me.

As I reflect on this story, I am aware that it is void of personal emotion. Even the description of the lashings of a whip in the first sentence conjure up a picture of a desolate man facing a wall, a dullness in his eyes, sunken cheeks, and not one twinge of pain with each snap of the whip against his back. This was, of course, on purpose, because to connect language to any emotions seemed a dangerous exercise for me back then. The closest and safest way to connect language to any emotions was to embed these hidden images in these types of stories. My rationalization was that when I felt safe I would and could go back to read these stories, inviting myself to explore the depths of my own pain and loss. Over time I would, but quite often just knocking on the door of my own pain and loss would be enough to overwhelm me.

This particular short story captured the fragmentation of my childhood journey. Time would pass and I would have no connection to it. Seasons would come and go and they would not register with me. Not only was I non-participatory with my youth I was disconnected from it as well. I wrote this piece to serve as a commentary on who I had become, some lonely and abandoned soul, wandering through the seasons of life without explanation and without purpose. The character in the story is not without hope but hopeful, lost perhaps but not disjoined. This thread of hope is expressed through the amount of detail that the character captures of what is going on around them. This served as another reflection of my life. An observer of life more times than a participant of it.

Expressing myself has always been a very controlled and protected process. I had great difficulty in opening up and being 'real' to someone. I became so obsessed with self-protection that I ended up creating a new identity in order to cope with what was happening in my life during a four-year period in particular. This new identity started in my grade six English class, where our teacher gave us a creative writing assignment. Before I knew it, I had brought to life this new person and it consumed me. I now was completely convinced that I was no longer Michael but instead my name was X15-QI. I was an alien.

In the following four years, I had chronicled my entire life as an alien including detail about my home planet, my adventures there, and how I came to be stuck on earth. I had myself so completely convinced of the fact that I was an alien that it took me rationalizing the impossibility of such a thing up until the end of grade ten before I dismissed it as fantasy. Now I can look back and find some humor in it - especially when I share this story with family and friends who have known me since a child, but during this time, it served to isolate me.

By the time I had managed to break free of this self-imposed identity, I was socially isolated and drawn back into my spiritual past with a renewed passion. By grade twelve, my lunch hours involved sitting around a table with a few other like-minded people, talking about such things as passing our hands through solid objects. We would share our spiritual experiences with each other and mock the simple-minded people that filled up the rest of the cafeteria, perhaps out of a need to self-soothe. Whatever the reason, I grew more and more distant from my peers, completely unaware of a growing internal disconnection from life.

The isolation came from the fact that I thought I was different from everybody else. As early as sitting on that sundeck with my mother, I felt set apart. During those early years, I found that I could not fit in and I was starting to be bullied quite often. For many years of my childhood, not a school day would go by without being targeted by someone and beat-up. Perhaps it was as simple as I was always the new kid on the block, having just moved to a new community and a new school. Either way, the bullies came in all sizes and numbers.

In one incident, a redheaded boy must have been a foot shorter than I was at the time, but had the support of about a dozen bigger people. They trapped me on my way back home one day, and after the little redheaded boy picked a scab off, forcing me to eat it, the boys there chocked me until I blacked out. I came to a few moments later, gagging and coughing. I got up, brushed myself off and got home late for supper. Whether it was being chased down the street by three older teens on bicycles while I was on foot, or thrown into lockers as I walked down a hallway, I was constantly being bullied.

The worst incident of bullying came one day after school. I had begun to walk a different way home, as cutting through the backfield left me with bruises and they were not from the shrubbery. I turned the corner after leaving the school parking lot and I looked at the top of the hill ahead of me. Slowly gathering at the top was a large group of students. I knew that they were there for me so I opted not to look for confirmation of my suspicion but instead to head down a different street. At that point, about fifty students became caught up in the mob mentality and chased me down. The crowd had broken into several smaller groups, running ahead to block off my escape. They had literally blocked off all of the streets and pinned me into a corner. I went home quite sore that day.

These early bullying experiences, accompanied by the pain of moving from school to school, and place to place, lead me to disconnect from what was happening around me. It became easier to process life's events if I was not aware of being present for them, either emotionally or cognitively. Thus, this pattern of existing in a non-existent way continued through my entire adolescence. As I became an adult this way of functioning was becoming more and more disruptive in every aspect of my life.

It was early in my marriage that I knew I needed to seek out some help because of my dissociative behaviors. It was now quite disruptive and becoming a strain on my relationship with my wife. The journey for me to a place where I no longer needed to use dissociative behaviors to survive was a long one. I was growing in my relationship with Jesus Christ, I was growing in my relationship with my wife, and I was learning accountability through the early relationship with my pastor. I was changing and becoming more and more the person I had always wanted to be. I discovered something quite profound through this journey, which continues to this day. Not only have I become the person that I had always wanted to be but I also discovered that I was already that person and had always been that person; only he had been buried under hurt, pain, and intense anger for so many years.

These earlier journeys all have contributed to who I am today. My acknowledgment of these experiences inform my awareness when speaking, and more importantly, when listening to others. My exploration of the emotional experience, seeking language to describe what I was feeling during these times helps to equalize my emotional capacity and my cognitive capacity. These early experiences comprise the foundation of my presuppositions and form the foundation of this book. These journeys and experiences are where the ideas around relational dynamics come from. I also believe they are helpful to you, the reader, in order to read and understand the concepts and language of Experiential Authority.

As I have already written, Experiential Authority is the act of imposing the Speaker's experience upon the Listener. Consequently, like the False Memory Syndrome that dominated headlines in the late eighties and early nineties, Experiential Authority can have just as catastrophic consequences when used on someone exhibiting dissociative behaviors. In the 1980s and spilling over into the early 1990s, therapists, working with their clients who exhibited a noticeable disconnect from both cognitive and emotive experiences, began to help their client 'reconstruct' fragmented memory. Because of many factors such as the methodology used (hypnosis in some cases), and a lack of awareness around the therapist's own presuppositions, the therapist was very directive with the client in memory reconstruction. The result ended up with an explosive amount of Satanic Ritual Abuse cases throughout the United States and gave rise to what was referred to as the False Memory Syndrome.

The result was thousands of clients had claimed that they had been ritually abused in secretive cults that littered the neighborhoods of USA. More times than not, these reconstructed memories would isolate a member of the client's immediate family or trusted family friend as the perpetrator of these violent and quite often sexual crimes. Many people's lives were ruined as a result of the client's reconstructed memories. It took a group of people, whose lives were severely disrupted by the allegations against them, to form a special task force of such in order to combat these constructed stories by the clients.

In the end, it was the frequency and consistency of the client's stories across America that helped the experts determine that the therapists had been overly directive in 'helping' their clients reconstruct memories. In other words, therapists had been sharing with one another their client's fragmented memories, and reading about the fascinating cases coming out of therapy sessions from their peers and coincidently more and more 'fascinating' cases began to appear everywhere. Finally, courts began to piece together this common denominator and determined that these therapists had been imposing these fabricated stories upon their client's fragmented memories. When the media picked this up, as fast as the phenomenon of

Satanic Ritual Abuse appeared in society it disappeared. Coincidently, the amount of reported cases in therapy dropped to almost none. These days to read about such a thing in case studies would be incredibly rare.

Dissociation, by application, fragments the Listener's experience, effectively severing connections in the brain to minimize harm or the related psychological impact from that harm. This is accomplished by disrupting the memory connections, where there is a cognitive-based memory piece, from the emotive-based memory piece. The result is that the Listener may have an emotional memory that is not yet understood because there is no supporting language, normally supplied through the cognitive functions of the brain. The Listener may also experience somatic responses to various environmental changes in the same way as well, without any idea why because of this disconnection in the brain.

Such a process of remembering can be quite frightening and disorientating for the Listener exhibiting dissociative behaviors. The greatest harm the Speaker can do in this moment is to take their own presuppositions of what is happening to the Listener and impose that explanation and associated language upon them. The reason why this imposing explanation can become so harmful is that the Listener experiencing these various disconnects may have some sense of fear and more times than not a sense of loss around their experience. This sense of fear and sense of loss creates a tendency to desire the experience being presented by the

Speaker, since it has a sense of completeness, or wholeness about it, and provides a way to make sense out of the Listener's disconnection.

The problem with taking on the Speaker's explanation is that most likely the Speaker is wrong. The Listener, being the one with the dissociative behaviors has ended up disregarding their own experiences, without taking the time to explore the emotional disconnects associated to their experience. The Listener has done this in an effort to find language to explain their experiences. However, the Listener takes the Speaker's experience on as their own, in order to find an explanation, and more commonly, an escape from their own fear and sense of loss.

Over time, this whole transaction will begin to feel like the Listener is wearing heavy, oversized clothes. These heavy, oversized clothes represent the External Identities presented by the Speaker and although they may come with messages of acceptance and affirmation, those messages are temporary. The harm associated with these External Identities is accentuated when the Speaker has woven language of worth and value into the process. The Listener has taken on these External Identities without realizing that those identities also come with worth and value measurements attached to the identities. In the end, the Listener will begin to feel even worse than they did in the beginning.

In this scenario there was no space

given to the Listener experiencing dissociative behaviors to explore language to describe their emotional experiences. The fragmentation experienced by the Listener makes space awkward at best and full of fear and anxiety at worst, which leaves opportunity for the Speaker. The Speaker, who is imposing their experience, and/or explanation of the Listener's fragmentation, then fills up the space immediately. From a place of shame, the Listener responds, fearful of their experiences, and eager to make sense of it all. The result is an identity that is not the Listener's. The Listener also has a connection to their worth and value being defined by the Speaker who imposed the identity upon them in the first place. Such a transaction leaves the Speaker with immense power and authority, while the Listener with the External Identity continues to be harmed.

It is possible that the Speaker is not meaning to create this harm when speaking. Experiential Authority is not only done through the malicious and intentional but can also occur through naivety and ignorance. Since the majority of us do not take the time to examine our own presuppositions and to be aware of our own biases, judgments, and other limiting factors to conversation, we tend to bring harm through our conversations more times than not. The following story will highlight how the Speaker's naivety and ignorance can bring about just as much harm to the Listener.

When I was a young boy, there was a

particular type of novel that I enjoyed reading. It was called, "Choose Your Own Adventure". There were many in the series, all involving a different plot and theme, yet the structure stayed the same. You would read a page or two and then you would be faced with a decision to make in the form of a question. You were normally given at least two options and depending on which option you chose, the story would take you to another page in the novel. On and on this would go until, based on your choices, the story would end, either happily or not so happily. When I think of conversations from the perspective of the structure of these novels, allow me to illustrate how the conversation would unfold.

As the Speaker enters into the conversation, the Listener will begin to share their story. As the story progresses, there will be opportunities to respond to what the Listener is saying. I refer to these moments as facts; times, events, details, people, all that might cause the Speaker to become curious, wanting to understand something more about any of those facts. At this moment, the conversation looks a lot like the choose-our-own-adventure novel. The reason why it looks like the choose-our-own-adventure novels is that at the moment of asking a question, the Speaker will need to make a choice.

Either the Speaker can base their question on an assumption, or they can choose to respond to what the Listener said. Allow me to unpack both for a moment. An assumption means that the Speaker's question will be directive, and formed out of their own experience, understanding, and ultimately judgment of the Listener. When I reflect on what it means for me to sit in conversation with another, I need to be aware of some assumptions that I have.

My assumptions could be the result of societal constructs around issues of morality as an example. Earlier in the book, I referred to the example of someone who had an affair. If I am having a conversation with the individual who had the affair, an assumption that I may have could be the result of how I have been influenced by the culture and society around me that dictates the displeasure in those who have affairs. In that case, I may be sitting in judgment of this person before I have heard them say anything.

If the Speaker were to choose to respond to what the Listener is saying (through reflective listening as an example) instead of assume, then it is important to note that the responding question is also directive. It is formed out of the Speaker's own experience, understanding, and ultimately judgment of the Listener. The responding question is rooted in the Speaker's presuppositions, of which they should be aware. In the Speaker's self-awareness, the responding question is asked tentatively, as in a reflection instead of the directive. This process will create the space for the Listener to agree, not agree, or offer a corrective that will help the both of them understand the story more.

In my case, some of the presuppositions that I bring to a conversation, and that I am aware about, is that the person(s) that I am sitting in conversation with has an intrinsic value and worth. This is important to note because our questions and interactions will tend to reflect this to the other person. I also operate from the point-of-view that all questions are directive and that it is impossible for someone to be completely objective. Therefore, there is a need to have a heightened sense of self during the conversation. This is not a focus on oneself as much as it is an awareness of how the Speaker's own stories are impacted by the Listener's.

If this was a conversation with a client, there is also an awareness, or an assumption, that I will begin most therapeutic conversations in a power stance. What this means is that there is a perception by the client that I hold the power and the control. Therefore, there exists the need for me to be intentional around issues of power in order to minimize or equalize the power differential between the client and myself. If this was a conversation outside of a counseling setting, then I am aware of other places of power that I may hold. There may be issues of power related to gender, race, vocation, place in society, economic place, and the list goes on. Being aware of one's Positional Authority in a conversation is a necessary part of equalizing the power differential that exists in any conversation.

If the Speaker chooses to ask an assumption question, (which is based on presupposed judgement), sometimes, like the choose-your-own-adventure novels, the Speaker will land on another 'fact'. The Speaker has assumed correctly, which can still be helpful and affirming for the Listener sharing their story. It is important to note, though, that just because something is helpful does not mean it is reflective of a correct methodology. What has happened in this scenario is not that the Speaker did something 'correct' but that their assumption, constructed out of what they heard the Listener say, just happen to reveal another 'fact'. This process could be akin to flipping a coin, trusting that every time you flipped the coin it would land on heads.

Therefore, an assumption does not always land on another 'fact' and perhaps more times than not, the one assumption will land on another assumption. All the while, these assumptions will continue to reinforce the power and control inequality. The result is that the Listener will end up experiencing what I have spoken of throughout this book, that being Experiential Authority. Therefore, even though the Speaker may not succeed all the time when they read a choose-your-own-adventure novel, the Speaker does have an opportunity to set up their conversations with the Listener for success. The Speaker can respond instead of assume, using reflective listening skills, because as the Speaker may have been told at some point in

their life, they know what happens when they
assume.

Chapter Eight Historical Relational Authority

If we were to be described by what was, what a shameful people we would be, but to be known as who we are, what a wonderful place to be.

When I was eighteen, I began what would be a fifteen-year career in restaurant management. Those first few months of being in management taught me a valuable lesson that has stayed with me ever since. In order to get respect you must earn respect. In my arrogance and self-righteousness, I would strut around that restaurant barking off orders and 'getting things done'. I was so successful in my work that the owners became very impressed with my ability and increased my responsibility. Soon I was making the final call on whether a new employee stayed or left. I felt very good about myself.

Unknown to me at the time, a problem emerged because of my increasing level of arrogance towards the staff. That problem was the growing resentment of the senior staff towards me. I did my share of the work, often working longer shifts, so that was not the reason for their resentment; it was my attitude. I deserved the position that I was in. I was good at the position that I was doing. I excelled in every way at what I was doing. The problem was I knew it, and being the stereotypical youth that I was, it went entirely to my head. I *demanded* respect from every employee in that restaurant. Then it happened. There was a showdown between two senior employees and myself. The confrontations took place on two separate occasions. One employee was the head cook and the other was the head server. Both were much older than I was and had been working at this restaurant for several years.

On one very busy day, the restaurant was completely full and this server and I were butting heads all morning. Finally, in a fit of exasperation, she stood in the middle of the restaurant, and using a stream of profanities, she proceeded to tell me off. I can still picture her standing there with a coffee pot in one hand and waving her other arm erratically as she turned blue in the face. This proved rather embarrassing for me, as I was not near her at the time, so she needed to raise her voice to have me hear her from across the restaurant. She completely ignored me after that until the day I left. I had lost complete respect with her and even though I tried to gain it back respectfully, all opportunity had been lost.

The second incident occurred a few weeks later in the kitchen, where I was commenting on the lack of kitchen productivity, as well as the inaccuracy of the orders going out. Again, there was a long line of profanities sent my way. With a spatula in one hand, and food in the other, the head cook told me where to go and it certainly was not anywhere in his kitchen. Fortunately, I had already learnt a couple of things. Unfortunately, I had not learnt to keep myself out of this situation in the first place.

I knew that I needed to earn this cook's respect. I knew that the only reason he did not want to listen to me was that he had never seen me at work in the kitchen. He must have felt that he was not going to take orders from some kid that did not even know his way around a kitchen. To combat this, over the next several weeks I took advantage of every opportunity to get into that kitchen and work alongside this cook. I made sure that I did the most unpopular jobs and that I worked twice as hard as anyone in there did.

I know that this cook took advantage of my desire to prove to him that I could cook, and consequently my time in that kitchen was a lot longer than needed. However, I learnt a valuable lesson through that entire experience, and I gained the respect of this cook in the process. I learned that, though I may possess the skills needed to lead, I still needed to earn their respect. It was my attitude and willingness to join them wherever they were at, helping them work through the issue at hand, which won them over. When I stepped up and did this first, they then actively submitted to my leadership and direction. I had finally earned their respect.

What was missing in my relationship with the head server was a mutual collaboration and respect. I had Positional Authority over her, yet I used my authority and the power that came with it unwisely. The result was that I had permanently destroyed this relationship. In the case of the head cook, I also went into that kitchen taking advantage of my Positional Authority, which did not go well for me, however, this time I was able to come alongside him and through collaboration, I was able to gain his respect and salvage that relationship.

My initial arrogance when I began at this restaurant continued to hamper my relationship with all the employees. Because of my initial actions as a new manager, word had gotten out to all of the employees that this is the type of manager I was – this was who I was. I tried to demonstrate my collaborative nature and although I had limited success, such as with the head cook, my relationship with the other employees remained strained. It seemed as though there was nothing I could do to change how the employees viewed me. I was still being measured by who I was and not by whom I had become.

Quite often over the years, being from smaller communities, I would run into my ex-employees. The result always seemed to be the same. Their interaction with me in the present was based on the last encounter they had with me. Because these were my ex-employees, most of the time the last encounter they had with me was a hard conversation that resulted in me terminating their employment. So, one can imagine how most of those interactions may have gone. What this looked like was that their description and interaction with me in the present was based on their knowledge of me and interactions with me in the past. They would do this even though we both had moved on and changed from that earlier encounter.

I had been a Christian for just over two years and was still an older teen when the senior pastor of the church I was attending decided to make me an intern youth pastor. At the time, I was already a part of the youth leadership, running a discipleship course and preaching occasionally. Our church was developing a training program for pastors and my pastor thought that this would be a great opportunity for me to go through. In essence, I became the guinea pig in order to try out this new chapter in the life of our church.

When I was approached about this, I enthusiastically embraced it and looked forward to when I could begin. It was announced in Church on a Sunday morning much to the joy of the congregation and I jumped right into my new role with a lot of energy. However, the only thing I had going for me was my charm, and even that was not so charming at times. My overall knowledge of the Bible was incredibly limited. I think I had only read the first five books of the Old Testament, and maybe three quarters of the New Testament. To compensate, I spent countless hours at the church learning and leading. As a result, I found myself getting more and more involved in the actual administration and board level at the church. Then it hit me. I became aware that I would be held accountable for my words and actions because of the role I was playing in influencing youth.

As I started thinking about this, I realized that I needed to get out of leadership. I had become so involved in the politics of the church, and the various administrative aspects, that I had lost the love that came with serving the youth. I was getting increasingly bitter and easily frustrated. Part of the symptoms, which helped me conclude that I needed to resign, was that during those few months that I was an intern youth pastor, my personal bible study and reading had all but diminished. As well, my personal prayer time was replaced with praying at the beginning of a service or when the offering was being taken.

I knew that I needed to get out so I went to the pastor to resign from the program. Regrettably, the pastor had placed too much value on the success of his program. Consequently, he neglected to recognize the fact that he should have never allowed me to be in the program in the first place. Because of the pastor's focus on the success of his program, he refused my resignation, and told me that I would have to talk to the board. I then approached the board, told them that I was not ready for leadership, and therefore wanted to resign. I went on to explain that my personal relationship with the Lord was weak and that I did not want to have the responsibility of the youth on my hands. I concluded that I should not be in leadership when there was still so much 'grounding' that I needed to do in my relationship with the Lord.

Unfortunately, the board refused my resignation, telling me instead that I was just young and that I would learn. I told them that I was still going to quit whether they accepted it or not, to which they became quite upset. It breaks my heart to talk about this but I actually had to leave the church entirely in order to get free from what the board was imposing on me. In a small town, this was a difficult decision to make as it meant leaving the intimate church community that I had found much affirmation in, all the while still working out my own relationship with God.

Unmindful to me at the time were the countless other issues that were present between the board and the pastor, and only a few months later the church went through a church split right after the board fired the pastor. This happened shortly after the pastor threw a hymnal at one of his elders. The elder had fallen asleep during one of the pastor's sermons. Unfortunately, the pastor missed and hit the elder's wife instead. My leaving the church was a hard leadership lesson for me to go through. I was still haunted by my decision to quit for the next year and a half.

In one particular incident, I had moved away from this town, and just happen to be back one week, visiting my parents, when the phone rang. A Christian man from that same church had tracked me down at my parent's home. He demanded that I pay him one hundred dollars for the damage done to his pool cover. It seems that the youth had gone and used his pool and in the process damaged the cover. I told him that I was no longer involved with the youth and his response shocked me. He did not care what I thought; the youth still recognized me as a leader and because of that, I needed to take responsibility for their actions and pay him the money. I refused and this man ceased talking to me.

I remembered these stories and others like it, as I was researching the various ideas around Experiential Authority. When I continued to take apart Experiential Authority in order to understand the new language that I had discovered, I examined the various relational dynamics connected to the concepts. In the exploration of the related concepts to Experiential Authority were other emotional experiences that needed language to describe them. What came out of the above-mentioned stories then, combined with similar stories throughout my life, was the language to describe an experience, which I have now called Historical Relational Authority.

Within the construct of Historical Relational Authority, there is a Speaker who knew the Listener at some point in the past, and had a relationship with them, who is now interacting with the Listener in the present. However, the Speaker is imposing an identity upon the Listener as it relates to the Speaker's perspective of the Listener, based in a historical context. One of the more common examples I have used in my teaching of this idea is the sensation of going to your twentieth High school reunion and having that experience of being back in high school once again.

There is an underlining idea behind most developmental theories that as individuals we are continuously growing, changing, and learning. As a result, because of this, those processes of change will influence how we act in the present, as compared to how we may have responded to something similar in the past. This new result comes because of greater knowledge or understanding of self, others, our surroundings, and a larger perspective on our environment. The end idea is that who you are in the present is not necessarily a reflection of who you were in the past.

Therefore, the act of Historical Relational Authority is to take a snapshot of how the Listener 'was, based on what they 'did', and transpose that external identity upon the Listener today. It would be like putting on some piece of clothing that the Listener wore pre-puberty. Chances are it will not fit. In the exploration of this new idea of Historical Relational Authority, I began to see emerging evidence of its effects in larger social systems. Historical Relational Authority is not limited to individual relational interactions but can also involve the idea that as a society the Speaker(s) tend to impose some constructed external identity upon each other all the time.

Perhaps this is a reflection of humankind's need to organize itself into societal constructs. It is this idea of examining what a person does and then assigning a predisposed identity to that person's actions. Even if the Speaker does not have a relationship with the Listener, the Speaker's actions will lead them to describe the Listener a certain way. Therefore, even if the Speaker has contact with the Listener later the Speaker will have referred back to their description of the Listener, based on what the Listener did in the past.

An example of assigning an External Identity is an animal rights activist. Even the title helps reinforce the External Identity that society has imposed upon this individual. When someone passionately speaks out about any particular topic, such as animal rights, society tends to have predetermined what type of individual that person might be. In this particular example, someone vocalizes and passionately speaks out against cruelty to animals, calling for change and for reform. Society may tend to equate some negative or positive descriptions of identity upon that person based solely upon the outward actions of the individual. What might happen if another person, who does not express themselves in similar ways, has a conversation with the first person – only to find out that they both share very similar points of view? Would that type of interaction influence or change the description of the External Identity? I suggest that it would.

Such a conversation would challenge what we would commonly refer to as a stereotype. In this type of interaction, even though the outward actions of both individuals may appear to be different we have discovered that they share similar points-of-view. In a healthy interaction, the perspective of each person is increased and we have come to know and understand each other in healthier ways. However, such is the power of stereotypes that their remains a desire to impose an External Identity upon another individual, based solely upon what you see and what you hear, even if the two do not necessarily correspond as in the example here.

The idea of stereotyping permeates culture and society and it is the Speaker's way of making sense of their surroundings. There seems to be a need to have the Speaker's world makes sense and so if stuffing the Listener into a box helps the Speaker to do that they are predisposed to doing so. To counteract this societal phenomenon, the Speaker can begin to be curious as to who this Listener is when the Listener does not fit into the box the Speaker has constructed for the Listener. This idea of separating a person's actions from who they are has now created enough space for a conversation to occur. In the space for a conversation, an opportunity is created to understand who the Listener is, which is no longer based on what they do. As a concept, this process is critically important to understand because it does two things for each of us.

The first thing it does is that it is helpful in showing the Speaker their own biases when it comes to the External Identities that they either place on people around them, or reinforce through their actions, based solely on the Listener's outward actions. The second is that it opens up the space for the Speaker to have a conversation with the Listener in order to understand who they really are. The most significant place that this concept can have the greatest impact is in any intimate relationship where there is conflict between two people. If, in the midst of the conflict, both parties can appreciate the difference between the Listener's actions versus the External Identity that the Speaker either has prescribed to the Listener or have reinforced between them both, the Speaker will immediately be setting up their relationship for success.

The reason that this sets up their relationship for success is that if the parties involved in conflict can minimize any associated cultural or societal identities related to the observed outward action, they can then become curious about who the person is and seek another perspective. This, then, can be followed by a greater understanding, which comes through communication and connection. In other words, each person becomes aware of the External Identities that either have prescribed to the other or have participated in. Through this open communication with one another, they have created space to challenge those very identities, which leads to discovering who they really are and more importantly who they want to be.

These ideas around societal-based External Identities are important in understanding how Historical Relational Authority works. It is important because of the Speaker's tendency to pass judgment upon the Listener is based on limited and quite often biased information about the Listener. Without an awareness of how they have been influenced by societal constructs (stereotypes), the Speaker can weave those descriptions together with their presuppositions when interacting with the Listener. Historical Relational Authority builds on such harmful interactions by introducing past relationships and intimate communities into the picture with a projected sense of how the Listener should be, which is in turn based on the Speaker's perception of who the Listener was at some point in the past.

If I break down Historical Relational Authority further, there are really three concepts intertwined and interconnected in such a way that the potential for harm exists. Like Experiential Authority, these three concepts come packaged by society in different types of relationships and for the most part are connected to the social norm. It is the idea that we do not need to look very far in order to find someone who is using Historical Relational Authority in our lives with us or with someone we know. Most people, driven by a need to understand, use this societal methodology of packaging up people into prescribed boxes with labels. People do this with each other, more times than not, based on limited historical interactions with one another. I will attempt to provide some common examples as I work through these concepts in order to help illustrate this idea.

The first concept is Historical, meaning that this idea, process, and power stance, is based in the significant past. I am referring to the idea of past being longer than the last year and so a Grad reunion is a great example of the Historical. Relational is referring to relationships, or meaningful interactions with other individuals, enough to register as a separate packaged event. In this example of a Grad reunion, those meaningful relationships may be one's close friends from their Grad class who may not necessarily be close to you now. The third concept is Authority, which speaks to the power differential that existed in that relationship in the past.

Power differential in of itself is a complex topic to unpack but in this example, I will simply share my presuppositions around power. First, I believe power to exist in every relationship. A description of power in a healthy relationship is the ability for both people to freely give and take this power. Second, I believe power to be an illusionary concept, replaced only by the perception of power. The idea around a perception of power is best illustrated when talking to a couple dealing with some problems and the therapist introduces the power language. Inevitably, both are inclined to state that the offending partner is the one with all the power.

Therefore, an expanded definition of Historical Relational Authority would look something like this. Historical Relational Authority is the phenomenon that occurs between two people in the present, where a pre-existent relationship has been established sometime in the significant past, and harm is done to the Listener, when the Speaker draws on that pre-existent relationship, utilizing a power differential, and imposes a narrow description of identity (connected to issues of worth and value) onto the Listener, out of that pre-existent relationship, reinforced through that power differential.

Here is my attempt to over-simplify this definition: Two people who meet up again, who knew each other well at some point in their significant past, and the Speaker relates to the Listener with old definitions of identity, utilizing power and control that the Speaker has in the relationship in order to impose those old definitions of identity. Historical Relational Authority is the idea that the Speaker knew the Listener twenty years ago and so that is not only how the Speaker is going to relate to the Listener now, in the present, but that is how the Speaker will view the Listener, interact with them, and interpret their actions in the present.

Therefore, if it was perceived that the Speaker had the power in their relationship with the Listener twenty years earlier, and the Speaker began to relate to the Listener in the present with these old definitions of identity, the harm that comes is a challenge to the Listener's sense of identity, value, and worth in the present. The Listener may have entered that conversation or interaction, confident in whom they had become, the ways they had changed, matured, and expanded in their understanding of who they are. However, because of the unique combination of these three concepts and the underlying power differentials at work, the potential is there to be harmed by that interaction.

To illustrate what I mean with Historical Relational Authority, I will share a story from my twentieth reunion. I was anxiety-ridden, nervous, and wondering what this Friday night 'meet and greet' would be like, considering I had not seen my classmates for these twenty long years. I had moved away from this city twenty years earlier and for me, everything had changed. Yet, in spite of feeling like I was a completely different person then I was twenty years earlier, I walked away from the evening feeling as if I was right back in High School, living out my teenage fears around acceptance, security, and attachment.

The evening did provide an interesting perspective from my place at the table. I was sitting across from my wife, who somehow was able to normalize the evening for me, keeping a healthy perspective on the evening's events. She also provided humorous commentary at times, all in an effort to keep me from laying down under the table in the fetal position, rocking myself back and forth for comfort. The reason for my anxiety was from the moment I entered the room, I looked for familiar faces, and as my eyes met the eyes of my fellow graduates, the responses I got were as if we had landed back in high school.

I was looking around the room at the fifty plus graduates that were celebrating this reunion. I noticed immediately that we had all gotten older, even if we were not acting older. Many of my classmates had not seen each for at least the last ten years, since the last Grad reunion. Now, in this room, and in this environment, it was if we all were transported back to some lonely day in Grade eleven, in the cafeteria of my old High School. Some, with spouses in tow, and others whose spouses were smarter than that and stayed home for the evening, began to culminate into the same social groups from twenty years earlier.

The one factor that helped this now anxious-ridden environment was that we were all twenty years older and knew how to shake a hand and offer pleasantries before shooing the person off in order to get back to each other's individual high school social group. In the midst of this environment, the memories of sitting in my high school cafeteria, talking with a couple others clad in black, wondering how to put our hands through solid objects came flooding back. I took my seat almost obediently, waiting for the lunch bell to ring.

Historical Relational Authority is the idea that even after twenty years the Speaker would look at the Listener and surmise them, based on how the Speaker related and understood the Listener twenty years earlier. This surmising, immediately gave the Speaker a place of authority over the Listener, which becomes a power-over stance. At one end of the relationship spectrum, this is not helpful, and toward the other end of the spectrum, it is ultimately quite harmful.

I suppose what this weekend experience really taught me was that Historical Relational Authority has more to do with the larger socio-cultural constructs that are imposed upon each other, then my classmates from twenty years ago who still think I am a dork for bringing a briefcase and wearing a suit to my first day of school in grade eight. I could remain shameful of my social awkwardness expressed on my first day of school in a new city or I could reflect on the reality that I was being treated in the present like that same individual from twenty years earlier. Any which way I frame it, the idea I am presenting here is that the concept of Historical Relational Authority is alive and well and is doing more harm than good.

I left that evening, and that experience, wondering how the evening would have played out if we did not have a twenty-year gap in relationship with one another. I wondered if I would have been hiding under the banquet table that evening, wishing these fellow classmates knew who I was today instead of then, if I had continued relationships with my classmates. Nevertheless, that was not the case. I had lost touch with them and for the most part, it had been twenty years. Therefore, instead of enjoying meaningful conversations and social interactions, I was observing a High School snub from my seat of insecurity.

Chapter Nine Power

Power exists in relationships. This power is woven into both our attraction of one another and our disgust of one another. It is called power because it is power, and there is no hiding that fact. I fear that those with power have convinced themselves of its innocence, its neutrality, and its inability to cause harm. I fear, that in the Speaker's desire to have power in a relationship, they may try to minimize any harm that the misuse of power may do to the Listener in order to contain and obtain the power for themselves. Power, therefore, is an intoxicating drug.

Nevertheless, like the power running through the wires in our house, power in relationships can both be helpful and harmful. Studying the power dynamics that exist in relationships led me to conclude that the use of power is one of give and take. At any given point, if power could be measured in a relationship, we may find that one person has more power than the other does. However overall, in an ideal relationship, the distribution of power has been equalized. This equalization of power represents a continuous giving back and forth of power with neither holding equal amounts of power at any given time. What makes it equal then is that both parties have agreed to the amount of power that either have in any given moment.

It is within this evolving, dynamic nature of relationships, that we will seek to understand how power works. The focus in a healthy relationship will be to achieve an equilibrium of power in which either partner choses what types of power they 'give' to the other and vice versa. Because power exists, but is illusionary in nature, it cannot be measured, only observed, when it comes to relational dynamics. In any relationship, each person decides what roles and functions they will take on at any given time. When both are satisfied with what they are giving and receiving in the relationship, healthy power equilibrium will be achieved.

Within this equilibrium, there will be positive themes of worth and value received and given. Each person's role and function will be done freely of themselves and will attempt to communicate worth and value to their partner. The affirmation of the person's role and function by their partner will then communicate worth and value back to the person. This continuous give and take in a relationship is fluid and constantly changing based on the circumstances of the moment. Because the power differential can change in the moment, this will affect the associated messages of worth and value. In order to understand how this works, let us look at the example where one partner is sick and is being cared for by the other.

In a healthy relationship, we can surmise that when the one partner is sick the other partner will change their role slightly to care for or 'nurse' their partner. In this scenario, there still exists a power equilibrium, because the person caring for their partner has chosen to do so. That loving act is communicating worth and value to their sick partner. On the other side, the sick partner receives the care well, thanking them, and communicating back worth and value to their partner who is caring for them.

If the caregiver begins to feel like their sick partner is getting better and surmises that they have the capacity to care for themselves, yet seems to still take advantage of the care being provided, the power is no longer equal. In this moment, the positive aspects of power are dissipating, along with associated descriptions of worth and value. These dynamics are occurring, even though on the surface it may appear that nothing has changed.

In fact, in that moment two significant changes have occurred. The first, and probably most important, has been recognition by the person caring for their partner that they have reached their capacity to care and now needs something to change in order to balance the power dynamic. They are beginning to feel like their sick partner is holding all the power. Consequently, the impact of the messages they are receiving from their sick partner around their own worth and value is decreasing.

The second significant change that may have occurred is not that the partner is no longer sick or 'faking' it because that may be presumptuous on the part of the caregiver. It is, rather, something that their sick partner did or said. This may be a nuance in verbal communication or in the sick partner's body language, that now very slightly communicates a negative message of worth and value back to the caregiver. It is entirely possible that the sick person is still sick and in need of continuing care, but how the sick person has communicated is changed, and that is what has influenced how the caregiver has now seen the relationship.

In this moment of frustration, if the caregiver were to reflect on how they were feeling, being careful to find the language to describe their emotional experience, it would open up the space for the both of them to seek that power equilibrium in their relationship once again. It is this important step of self-reflection, and the associated awareness of one's emotional state that is often overlooked in relationship communication. What this reflective moment does is provides opportunity for the caregiver to find the language to describe what they are feeling. In response, their sick partner can utilize reflective listening skills in order to understand the other's experience of caring for them.

The Speaker cannot contain power in a relationship. The Speaker cannot own it either. I find this ironic, because my observation of human behavior shows that as a society, we work so desperately hard to contain that power, to hold it close to ourselves. Power exists to serve a function and is beyond the Speaker's reasoning, desire, and grasp. Even when the Speaker is freely given power, the Speaker somehow loses sight of the fact that as easily as the power was given, it can be taken away. Ultimately, the tangible aspects of power are illusionary. Power, existing in a relationship, is a metaphor more than an actual concept. It is the easiest way that we can understand the mutuality and interplay between two people, or in another setting, help us characterize leaders and their followers.

Power, then, is this idea of taking and giving of authority, a hierarchical structure outlining a relationship at any given moment. Power is the vehicle in which we use when we want to either drive or be a passenger. So if this understanding of power can be easily taken away, why does it seem so hard to overcome when a person with power is harming us through its misuse? Why, when in the moment the Listener is feeling the harmful effects of power's misuse, does the Listener not simply take power away or speak to its illusionary hold it has over them? This is where the harmful use of power in a relationship ties back to Experiential Authority. Within this harmful interplay of the use of power in the relationship, it is the Fear Perspective, which is perpetuating the harm. It is the confusion between acknowledging the Listener's own stories of loss and pain and the accepting of the External Identity pushed upon them by the Speaker.

The answer to my question, referring to the illusionary power holding so much control over the Listener, is best explained through something I refer to as Positional Authority. Positional Authority refers to those individuals who would be, by way of their position, given authority by some external means, and through that context begin to misuse the power that came with their position. The easy explanation to the harm that comes through the misuse of Positional Authority would be to say that the Speaker began to misunderstand power. Although that may be the case for about the first few minutes, given all that we know about the dynamics of relational power, I have a hard time convincing myself of the misunderstanding defence.

Instead, power is an intoxicating drug that screams affirmation and makes outlandish promises. It captivates our hearts, fogs our minds, and dims our spirits until we embrace it and drink from its fountain. A little over the top perhaps but I have tasted it and I have danced with it. So intoxicating it has been, that I am sure I was an ass for a lot longer than I was a nice guy. Power was not something I gave up easily and thankfully is something that I focus on trying to be aware of nowadays as to avoid that temptation again. In fact, if I find that my relationships are strained, it has become an automatic reaction of mine to examine my use of power in that relational dynamic. I am aware through my own experiences that it is too easy to fall into the lure of power. Even when you write about it, talk about it, and think about all the harm that it does, one can easily fall into its clutches once again.

In my experience, I find that the biggest lure of power is the affirmation that it brings. This power affirmation enhances the Speaker's individuality, speaks to their specialness, and values their opinion. Through this affirmation the Speaker is blinded by the fact that it does all of that at the expense of everyone else around them. Although we may value our individuality, we are still seeking intimacy and acceptance within community. Therefore, when the Speaker finds that they have Positional Authority, it has the effect of one given a special ticket, which allows them to go to the front of the line. Power calls the Speaker out and shines a spotlight on them, and the Speaker can easily fall victim to power's lavish promises of worth and value.

In power's illusionary act, the Speaker is affirmed in their individuality. The Speaker is made to feel special through the recognition of the power they 'contain', and the Speaker believes they are being affirmed and accepted within community. The Speaker accepts these gifts of affirmation and believes this acceptance, even though the use of this power normally comes through the expense of those very people in that community. There is a personal responsibility to those who have been given power through Positional Authority, because this power is freely given, instead of historically taken. With power freely given comes responsibility, and when the intoxication of power takes over, no amount of passive descriptions are going to minimize the harm that will inevitably follow.

As much as the 'innocent' fall victim to the lure of power in relationships, and its promises of worth and value, there is a paradox here. The paradox comes when the Speaker's desire to gain a sense of worth and value in a relationship does so by seeking out the power in that relationship. Meanwhile the Listener, who is being harmed by the misuse of power in a relationship, is choosing not to speak out against that power because of their same desire to gain a sense of worth and value. These are the underlying ideas of Experiential Authority, where the Listener takes on the External Identity presented by the Speaker, in hopes of affirming the Listener's own ideas around worth and value. However, ultimately the Listener finds that those very same ideas of worth and value are now defined by the one with the power, namely the Speaker.

Our worth and value is something that cannot be measured through human means. It is appalling to me that we try, because our attempts are limited to our own experience with various expressions of measurement containing power and authority. We are further limited to contextual, cultural, and societal constraints when attempting to ascribe measurements for one another's worth and value. Therefore, I believe that our worth and value is intrinsic and consequently immeasurable by human standards. No matter if you are an atheist, an agnostic, a humanist, or a Universalist, the teaching around the intrinsic nature of worth and value is present in each of them.

From each of these sources of understanding, it is understood that our intrinsic worth and value is measured beyond one's own ability, position, or accomplishments. It is simply beyond our ability to construct any standard of measurement that would come close to measuring one's worth and value. Though the monetary value of an individual has been measured scientifically, as in organ donation, or socially, as in the slave trade, these were contextually assigned values, which have changed with time. The reality is that we are not able to place a measurable and determined value on anyone.

In our attempts to define and measure the worth and value of each other we find that quite often worth and value are seen in contrast. One's worth is measured as more, when another's worth is devalued. This comparison to each other – this assignment of worth and value – is quite often viewed as a measurement that one is more, and by the same definition, one is less. This societal constructed definition is seen in the economic definitions of people, religious definitions of people, and cultural definitions of people – just to name a few. It seems only when we move beyond ourselves are we able to appreciate we do have an immeasurable worth and a worth that does not come at the expense of another's worth and value.

In order to appreciate our immeasurable worth we need to push through the societal thin, imposing, and external identities used to describe our worth and value. We need to see past these imposing barriers so we can begin to see that we do have a worth and value that is beyond ourselves and more importantly, beyond our attempts to create worth and value for ourselves. These imposing barriers are what make Experiential Authority so damaging. They package an illusionary message of worth and value, at the expense of discarding one's own experiences around worth and value, for the External Identity thrust upon them.

Ironically, once the Listener accepts this External Identity in an attempt to find their embedded sense of worth and value, the Listener begins to feel an erosion of that very same worth and value. This erosion occurs because the Listener has discarded their own experiences – the very thing that makes them who they are. The irony here is that the Listener's messages of an intrinsic worth and value are embedded in their own experiences and in the unspoken emotional language that accompanies those experiences. Therefore, in the Listener's efforts to secure a worth and value for themselves from the Speaker's External Identity, the Listener has overlooked the fact that those messages were there all along.

The tragedy of the religious community occurs when our attempts to secure a sense of worth and value for ourself is exploited and manipulated using Experiential Authority. My personal conviction is that the unspoiled message of one's worth and value should come from this very same religious community. My reason is because I believe it points towards the recognition of being created, and is an invitation to worship the Creator, because of the joy and love expressed through the Creator's creation of us. Worth and value as expressed through God's creation of us is a relationship that surpasses humanity's faults and our own limited abilities.

However, conformity and change have become, in so many ways, the entrance fee to the Evangelical Church and to safe community under the steeple. This is such a high price to pay when my Evangelical-based theology teaches me something different. Nevertheless, I cannot turn this into a theology-based critique upon the Church and indeed such complicated arguments are not necessary here. Instead, the simple explanation comes through those ideas of conforming and changing.

I would like to parallel these ideas of conforming and changing in a church community to the ideas describing a relationship. When two people enter into an intimate relationship, based on mutual care and respect, there are a few similarities between what that relationship should look like, and what I am describing here. The two people have come to enjoy each other for who they are, what they are, and the curious attractions that follow. They work hard to create a safe place for each other, and in those intimate times of sharing, they are free to explore feelings and thoughts without fear of reprisal or rebuke.

The mutuality of this relationship means that over time, both individuals will slowly adapt and change in order to meet each other's needs and wants to the best of their ability. This change is not demanded but is given out of a place of mutual love and respect for one another. In the same sense there is a conformity that occurs, described by external factors with such pithy things as, "Don't they look like a cute couple" or even in a mutual recognition of the blending of similar tastes and values. At no point during the life of this relationship – if it has remained in a healthy state – has either of the individuals lost their individuality. They have responded to each other out of a place of caring, love, respect, and honouring – all ideas surrounding the great thoughts of worth and value.

However, when I look at the Church, sometimes I find that upon entrance to this 'safe place' a sign exists at the front door demanding change and conformity before entrance to this community is allowed. These ideas are brought home even more succinctly when the pastor shares how the Lord found him in his brokenness and sin. Then, instead of extending that same grace, or creating the space in which the participant in this community can explore what that relationship might look like, an ideology is presented instead. The pastor, after having found measurable success through their own experience, and being aware of the authority that the pulpit provides them, begins to present their experience to the congregation.

The intimacy of this community invites the Listener to trust what is being shared. Therefore, in this context, the Positional Authority that the pastor has been given, affords the pastor the opportunity to project their experience of achieving righteousness as being the correct experience. It is within this idea of intimate community, where a common external factor draws them together, that Experiential Authority has space to flourish. Of course, Experiential Authority can be found anywhere, but in such a setting, where there is not an awareness of the Positional Authority and power that is given to the Speaker, there is a tendency to push these External Identities upon the Listener.

It seems that within a religious setting, there is the common belief that everyone there is part of this intimate community of believers, with the authority coming only from God. However, I believe that because of this presupposition, those who are typically set apart as the leaders of such a community, such as its pastors, are normally not initially aware of the Positional Authority and associated power that is freely given to them from the participants of this community. Initially, therefore, ignorance as to the harm that can come through the misuse of Positional Authority is present. However, that ignorance can be short-lived and within short order many different 'leaders' within this type of community may seek to take advantage of their Positional Authority.

Let me illustrate this with a story from the same church where the pastor whom I entered into an accountability relationship with was pastoring. In the fall of 1998, I had the opportunity to go to a conference in Kamloops, through my pastor, that featured a prominent Christian Speaker and author. After the conference my pastor asked me to share about this experience in church the following Sunday. Things were getting quite difficult in our church, as there seemed to be some mumbling and grumbling against the pastor's leadership. Because of those dynamics, I was very nervous about sharing with the church so I ended up writing out the entire experience. The next Sunday morning, I got up to share. I ended up staring at this piece of paper, reading every word quickly, until I was done. I got down and went back to my seat, careful not to look anyone in the eye.

The pastor got back up, thanked me for sharing and then asked the deacon present to pray for the offering. The deacon got up from where he was seated near the front, went up to the pulpit, and in front of the church proclaimed that this church does not agree with what I had just shared. I was shocked. I did not know what to do. I just sat there in complete disbelief while the song played for the offering. As this deacon made his way to me, he smiled as he put his hand firmly on my shoulder, squeezing slightly, before continuing. I wanted to leave but I stayed. I wanted to say something but I did not. A few months later the board asked the pastor to leave. I decided that it would be best for my family to leave as well. My wife and I joined a bible study hosted by another church, eventually ending up attending there instead.

The pastor leaving had nothing to do with what I shared that Sunday morning. When I inquired, it was the opinion of the board that it was bad enough that I had submitted to the pastor's leadership and that I had shared that I was accountable to him, but to say so in front of the church was just silly! I was told that I was simply a young man, ill informed, and obviously deceived through the words of this man. The deacon's wives found it necessary to phone up my wife and let her know just why we were wrong to follow the pastor. The deacons found it necessary to hold secret meetings to tell the church why any of us should not follow the pastor. It seemed like my sharing on that Sunday morning in affirmation of the pastor's ministry was what caused the wife of the head deacon to instruct the deacon on duty to go back to the nursery, so her husband could address the congregation and correct me in my experience.

Within this church there were many individuals abusing Positional Authority to impose their sense of what should be upon others. Certainly, the deacon's wife took advantage of her relationship to her husband in order to put me in my place. The deacon followed suit by coming up to me as he was taking the offering and placing his hand on my shoulder. As I examine this event from the present, I can also see how the pastor was using my experience of the conference in order to give a message to the dissenters sitting there on that Sunday morning.

The pastor used his Positional Authority to have me act in a particular way. Both the deacon and his wife also used their Positional Authority to have me act in a particular way. No wonder my wife and I felt disorientated with what was right and what was wrong. We had not had the space in this small church congregation to explore how we were feeling and what those emotions meant, as there were many individuals who were taking advantage of their Positional Authority in which to create harm.

Several years had passed since my wife and I had left this church. We spent several years in a great church environment and then when we moved to another province for me to finish my Master's degree. It would be a few more years when we ended having to leave another bad church experience. Upon reflecting on that experience, my wife said, and I quote, "In their view each person has value only inasmuch as they can conform and change - they love the potential, not the person." I was struck by how succinctly she had captured the essence of Experiential Authority within the Evangelical Church.

Chapter Ten Not-knowing

It is an observation of mine that the Speaker will tend to speak out of their experience more than their academic understandings. This place of experience is where they would connect with people, through mutually shared events, and unfortunately, when the Speaker is in a place of authority, this is where they can potentially do the most harm. It would make sense that the Speaker's personal experiences would be a natural place in which to connect with others. Out of this type of knowledge, the Speaker would share mutual experiences, similar likes and dislikes and can easily find affirmation and acceptance from the people. However, when the Speaker's personal experiences becomes experiential knowledge, and consequently the place where they derive truth, it can bring harm to vulnerable relationships.

The Speaker would take their experience of something, processed individually, and then filter it through their own presuppositions and previous experiences. The Speaker then allows that experiential knowledge to define a new sense of morality and truth for themself. Without that very important collaborative piece, which I refer to as the academic, the experience the Speaker has accumulated is elevated to a level in which they will dispense as being truth.

When the Speaker takes this new 'truth' and imposes it upon others, it becomes

Experiential Authority and it causes harm. The Speaker has personally derived worth and value from their experience, and now they are inviting the Listener to take on the Speaker's experience as theirs. Consequently, this invites the Speaker into defining the Listener's worth and value through that External Identity. I believe there is a balance that the Speaker can use in order to find some harmony between their experience and their academic understandings, which will not result in bringing harm to the Listener.

Instead of bringing harm to the Listener, the Speaker can use their understandings and presuppositions to guide their experience. This in itself is a journey, which should occur outside of any authoritative relationship. The process of experiential learning is to receive collaborative knowledge, the academic, and then go away and test that knowledge through experience. This type of experiential knowledge thickens the academic, which the Speaker would normally bring back to the collaborative community where they first learned it, in order to share what they have now experienced.

Within this collaborative community, the Speaker would then share their experiential knowledge tentatively, seeking feedback from the whole. This back and forth process enriches and reinforces the truth of the knowledge, which is then shared by the whole community as both experiential and academic. This newly acquired experiential knowledge will need to be verbalized, acted upon, and tested before the Speaker can own it as academic. At this point, this new experience will begin to tear down the Speaker's presuppositions. The result of this process should lead the Speaker to end up in a place of not-knowing.

Why not-knowing? Not-knowing allows the Speaker to be curious with the Listener, providing space for expressions of worth and value to be seen and heard. It is this provision of space, which ultimately is the end goal of not-knowing, that should be the focus of the Speaker. Expressions of worth and value may be tentatively offered up by the Listener as they explore their own experiences around worth and value. The Speaker will also have their own ideas around worth and value. Those ideas may have been helpful to the Speaker but may not be helpful to the Listener. In a harmful use of Experiential Authority, in order to project the Speaker's experience as the only experience, because of the individualized meaning that it holds for the Speaker, they will have closed down that space for the Listener to explore meaning around their own worth and value.

This harm comes about, not because the Speaker is without knowledge or without helpful experience, but instead it revolves around an idea. It is the idea in which that the Speaker recognizes that they are the only authority, instead of part of a collaborative conversation with the Listener. In a place of not-knowing, the Speaker would acknowledge that their experience is shared as one piece of a collaborative conversation instead of being the only experience and authority. This will then open up space to listen to the Listener's experience. This is possible to do as the Speaker, even if the Speaker is in a place of Positional Authority.

The Speaker may even be considered an expert and can speak with commanded authority, however, the moment the Speaker shares their experience with its related worth and value as the only authority, the Speaker has ended up harming the Listener. As the Speaker, they must approach their own experiences and knowledge with an appreciation that the Speaker is one member of a community and not the keeper of the truth. The Speaker must remain open to the idea that there still may be more to contribute to the Listener's experience and by association the Listener's related concepts around worth and value.

If these elements are in place then a trusted partnership between the Speaker and the Listener is what comes out of a place of not-knowing. Each shared piece of information holds meaning, even if it does not connect to the Speaker's experience. If this collaborative relationship is to succeed and be of mutual benefit then the final element that must be in place is that the Speaker must already have the presupposition that the Listener has immeasurable worth and value that goes beyond anything that the Speaker can ascribe to the Listener.

The Speaker must also speak from a

place of accepting that one's emotional capacity and cognitive capacity are equal and need to be listened to from that same place of equality. The Speaker must conclude that even though they may have formal training and experience, they are still only one voice in many. In conclusion, although the Speaker may have an authority, it is not theirs to exploit at the expense of the Listener's own experience.

This does seem to be a bit of a challenge since generally, people tend to share experiences as authoritative. In other words, since it happened to them or to someone they know, then it must be true. Of course, they are right in the most post-modern of ways, meaning it was true for them. Nevertheless, somewhere along the line it seems that the individualistic truth has replaced the meta-truths, and this is simply wrong. This is best illustrated when another speaker involved in this collaborative conversation between the first Speaker and the Listener offers his or her own experience as truth. Now we have lost collaboration and have introduced conflict.

There is an aspect of this interesting situation that I would like to focus on for a moment. I believe that the Speaker wants to be heard. The Speaker wants to be validated. I believe that this is a part of their longing for community and this is a very normal thing. In fact, I believe that the Speaker's desire for community is part of their essential self, something that lies at the very core of who we are as human beings. We were created for community primarily. When experience is shared, I am hearing a Speaker who wants to be heard and who wants to be validated. I am hearing a Speaker who wants to be a part of community. Therefore, if we do not take the time to hear the Speaker, that Speaker is sure to take a defensive stance, perhaps out of self-protection, or hurt, or loss, but in any sense we end up with conflict.

We begin life seeking healthy attachment, a desire to bond, and a curiosity of our surroundings. We then move into ego development, gaining a sense of self in relation to our world around us. Woven into this journey is the development of our morality, heavily influenced by various family systems and the intimate communities that we belong. The commentary on this individualized development of the person is varied and culturally poised when the outcome is compared to the journey. This commentary turned critique reveals that many of us have an underdeveloped sense of morality, an overdeveloped sense of ego, and relatively unhealthy attachment styles. The critique is observational and experiential in nature and reflects mass media and other North-American based commentaries.

It would seem that our adolescent journey into emerging adult-hood has left its scars. Perhaps it is the deconstructed family unit, which has left these youth without a sense of identity or sense of attachment. Perhaps it is the disconnection to past generations, hampered and strained because of the pace of technology. Perhaps it is the unchecked and untested results of a post-modernistic society, deconstructing the modernistic social structures but neglecting to reconstruct something in its place. At any rate, the result is this stagnated morality, which is illustrated by a black and white pitted sense of justice only as it seems to relate to self. In whatever way that we all got to adulthood it seems that we have all arrived without understanding the healthy aspects of power, control, and authority.

I certainly fit into this critique. In Grade 7, there was a substitute teacher in for my art class on one occasion. I had completed the project assigned and felt quite good about it until this teacher pulled out my offering from the rest and began to criticize it. His sense of comparison, drawing out what was wrong with my project without offering a corrective, but instead having it serve as a lesson to others – don't be like Michael – got me upset. In response to his insensitivity, I vaguely remember lecturing this teacher on his inexperience in teaching and how using critical comments to motivate a class was not helpful and was actually harmful. The result was me ousted to the hallway.

In Grade 8, my woodwork teacher pulled me out of the class and into the hallway after my attempt to bring some sort of control and structure to the classroom seemed to upset the teacher. His words to me as he held the top part of my arm with his firm grip was that the world does not revolve around me. In reflection, I was wondering if he was reacting to my organizing my peers to help complete my woodworking projects. Or perhaps he had heard how I organized my fellow classmates in my home economics class to complete the big sewing project for me without me ever having to do one stitch.

In Grade 11, I had a run-in with another art teacher. This time the teacher was a year or so away from retirement instead of a substitute teacher fresh out of University. On one particular day, he decided to attack a fellow student, verbally tearing them apart in front of the rest of the class. I rose from my seat and began to launch into quite a speech on his misuse of power and authority and the harm that his words were bringing to this young girl. My speech is far more developed now in the description of these concepts around misuse of power as I suspect my adolescent language back then was more rudimentary in its delivery. Once again the result of such an encounter had me not only tossed from his class but the teacher petitioned to have me thrown out of school.

It would seem that the ideas that I write about now have been percolating within me for my entire life. I present these examples in the context of me rising up against the tyranny of those who desire to misuse their authority and power. However, it is safe to say that I was allured by power's illusionary promises, and consequently misused authority and power wherever and however I could. Nevertheless, the contrast here is that in these examples of speaking against the misuse of Positional

Authority, I was called rebellious. In fact, it was and has been quite characteristic in my life that the only times I would have been called rebellious has been when I have risen up in similar situations and spoke out against the blatant misuse of power and authority. Even when I decided to start drinking while underage and attending parties out in the bush with my peers, none of those actions, curiously, were characterized as being rebellious.

In the context of Experiential Authority, I also find this rebellious language being used in similar ways. It comes through the various External Identities being imposed upon the Listener by the Speaker. The Listener is forced to either vehemently oppose the identity being forced upon them by the Speaker, which has the appearance of rebellion in society, or they reluctantly put on the identity. This comes with the sensation of constantly being uncomfortable with how it fits, all in the name of seeking approval and affirmation from the Speaker who first imposed upon the Listener this identity. The result is a mess, and in order to survive, the Listener becomes submissive to the Speaker who is abusing their authority. During this process, the Listener will end up forming unhealthy attachments to the Speaker in an effort to security affirmation and acceptance.

Within the last few years, I was seeking a men's group to join. I was invited by a work colleague to attend one such group that was held at his church each Wednesday morning. When I arrived with my colleague at my first meeting, there were nine other men, whom all had known each other for quite a while. I afforded myself the luxury of sitting in the background watching and studying everyone around the table. In this context, I could begin to measure whether or not this group would be a safe place for me to be and participate in. Early into the meeting, one man caught my attention. He was a bigger man, who had positioned himself at the head of the table that we were sitting at. The volume of his voice had me wonder whether he liked the sound of his voice more than his need for volume so everyone could hear. His gestures and body language were large; forming a psychological barrier, that no one could cross.

Given that his back was to the door behind him and he sat at the head of the table watching the rest of us, I could not help but begin to feel a bit trapped by his presence. I had concluded that this man must be the one 'in-charge' of this group. Quick introductions were offered and he led off, explaining that the Senior Pastor, who is normally the leader of this group, was away this week so he would be leading. Again his body language and gestures seemed to spell out the words, 'naturally, of course' in the air. Right from the beginning of this meeting, I became fascinated with his use of Experiential Authority. In particular, I was drawn to how he used humour in which to perpetuate the harm associated with Experiential Authority.

In a group setting, the Listener tends

to be far more vulnerable and insecure as compared to a more intimate one-on-one setting. This may seem contradictory to some; however, as a societal observation of North American culture, people are insecure in groups. Within a group, the Listener is prone to do self-comparison and struggle with the various insecurities that would arise from their conclusions. The Listener will become aware of the language used and their ability to pace with the flow of conversation. Likewise, the Listener will become focused on what is being discussed as a group, measuring it against their ability to participate or contribute to the group in order to gain acceptance. The result is that the Listener has become vulnerable and reacts to opportunities or gestures of acceptance without much thought as to whether the Listener agrees with the content. The end result is confusion for the Listener at best and quite harmful at worst.

In the above-mentioned example of this small group, this speaker would turn to another participant in the group, making a loud enough comment, entwined with his own laughter, so that the entire group could hear, disrupting the flow of other's conversations. He would then 'invite' the person he was looking at to join him in laughter. To not laugh with him at that moment would surely be seen as obnoxious or even confrontational. It is the look-right-at-the-person, followed by the person laughing at his or her own humour, which seemed so remarkably out of place. What is wrong with this picture? I concluded that what was wrong was the person did not laugh back, for that split second they took in the situation. Then, they awkwardly participated with this invitation to laugh, not-knowing that to do so was actually handing over power and control to the person laughing. Why is this so wrong? This seems like a mountain out of a molehill.

Perhaps, but it seemed out of place. It seemed so dirty. It is the context that is bothersome and not necessarily that this person's attempt at some humour is rather off the mark. This person is a recognized leader, and enjoys the authority that comes with being the leader. This person's stories seemed to indicate that they get to enjoy that authority in most every setting they are a part of. There was this air of expectation that commanded obedience from his audience and for him not to receive it would probably bring a shock to his system. This person had an ideology that was a part of their leadership and permeated everything that they did. There ideology was that the combination of their experience and knowledge made them an expert in their position. It was a classic - they were right - so the Listener needs to watch, listen, and be awed by their experience. Humour was their weapon of choice, which perpetuated that ideology. This is the basis of Experiential Authority.

Experiential Authority occurs when this Speaker takes their ideology, or experience, and presents it in such a way that their experience becomes the truth. This is coupled with the expectation that the Speaker has for the Listener, which is to meld and shape the Listener's experience in order to match the Speaker's. An extreme example of this might be a Speaker who makes a racist comment, laughs about it, while 'inviting' the Listener to participate with the laughter. In this group was a charismatic humorist that has a following and the adoration of many. All indications are that they are a great leader indeed. Why not strive to be like this leader. Why not emulate their characteristics, and apply their techniques? Where is the harm?

The harm is subtle and that is what makes Experiential Authority a difficult concept to unpack. The danger in this process is the devaluing of the Listener's own experiences, their own contributions, and their own expertise. If there is no invitation to collaborate then there is a teacher and a student, a learned one and an ignorant one, and a knowing person and an unknowing person. Even this framework would be acceptable if the teacher who knew, taught, or led, would draw out and build upon the student's own experiences. This way there would be created space within the student to assimilate the material, and not regurgitate, becoming a clone of the teacher at the expense of self. It is this step that seems to be missing, the step of creating space, and in fact was missing in this humorous didactic. It was missing because the Speaker had a purpose.

That purpose was to convince the Listener they were looking at to laugh, and therefore assimilate the very concepts the Speaker was conveying through the weapon of laughter. It was a weapon, because of the social dynamics going on. The Listener was stripped of their ability to choose and honour self in this process. If the Listener did not laugh, they ran the risk of being labelled and shunned by the group. The Listener was forced to laugh and in so laughing, the Listener agreed to change their own experience in order to match the Speaker's experience, thus affirming the Speaker and perpetuating the harm. Once again, I had found a negative example of Experiential Authority. I was discouraged because it was now embedded within the use of humour. Must I be suspect of laughter now? Such was a distressing place to be and I was stuck in terms of trying to explain a healthy aspect of any of these concepts.

As hard as I could, I simply could not find the language to describe what a healthy aspect of Experiential Authority and Historical Relational Authority looked like. My wife offered some helpful terminology, wondering whether Murray Bowen's explanation of differentiation might be an outcome experience that I was looking for. However, that seemed to structural, to defined, and to set in a system, mostly defined by family-of-origin, and not so applicable across community systems, cultures, and time. We both talked at some length about this and I laid it to rest for another day.

Certainly some of the positive ideas behind Historical Relational Authority are to become differentiated between who we are and what we do. Another way of saying this is to have an awareness of self that helps you identify the differences between who you are and your outward actions. Within this awareness of self, there is a difference, and an important difference. When left unchecked and unnoticed, a lack of differentiation perpetuates stereotypes, encourages External Identities, and fosters misunderstandings wrapped in conflict.

However, what I needed was language to describe the emotion related to the positive uses of power and authority. I did not want this book to perpetuate the idea of emotive equality but then reason it all away with cognitive constructs. Several months would pass before I was able to discover the emotive language needed to bridge the gap between the negative aspects of Experiential Authority and its positive counterparts. I once again turned back to Dr. Bréne Brown's work on shame and vulnerability. Here is a quote from Bréne Brown's book, "I Thought It Was Just Me" who in turn was quoting June Price Tangney and Ronda L. Dearing's book, "Shame and Guilt",

> "With increasingly complex perspective-taking and attributional abilities, modern humans have the capacity to distinguish between self and behavior, to take another person's perspective, and to empathize with other's distress. Whereas early moral goals centered on reducing potentially lethal aggression, clarifying social rank, and enhancing conformity to social norms, modern morality centers on the ability to acknowledge one's wrongdoing, accept responsibility, and take reparative action. In this sense, guilt may be the moral emotion of the new millennium."

The consensus from these researchers, Brown included, is that shame can have no positive attributes. This assertion around the negativity of shame left me wondering about the aboriginal communities that practice what I have come to understand as 'shaming circles'. When I was putting together a Restorative Justice Program for my home community some years ago, I learned how our aboriginal neighbors treated one of their community members who had harmed a neighbor in some way. The community would gather, along with the elders, the victim, and the offender, and would sit in a circle. Each person in the community would take some time to explain to the others how the actions of the offender affected them, even though they may not have been directly impacted by the offender's actions.

The victim is given time to explain how they were also impacted. Then the offender is given an opportunity to address their community. The hope is that the offender would feel what was described to me as 'shame' and would ask to be restored to the community. I found this imagery to be a powerful picture of what we could have in a non-aboriginal setting. However, it was somewhat idealistic because, unlike the aboriginal communities that I was neighbours with, the sense of community and family connections within my community were not as strong as it was within these aboriginal communities. This was a loss to me, and I processed it as such. The best that we could hope for was a restoration - the offender to the victim, and although this was still helpful, I felt that much was lost in the process.

It would seem that modern research is telling us that the use of shame is not helpful - useful perhaps for short-term compliance to community expectations, but easily broken down and unsustainable. I believe the reason for this is what Tangney and Dearing were explaining in their book. I think it is helpful, perhaps, to summarize what they are saying by stating that shame does not work in the ways it once did. This is not because we have achieved a higher state of morality, but perhaps because as a people we are now far more individualized then our ancestors.

This is probably a bit different perspective then what the authors had intended, however I think helpful for what I am discussing here. It seems sad to me that as a people, those classified as 'Western' in culture and philosophy, we have lost that sense of community, which we once had. I believe this is also attributing to the diminishing success that these aboriginal 'healing circles' are having with their members. I speculate that the diminishing success has been the dominant permeation of 'Western philosophies' into traditional Aboriginal teachings. Whether we like it or not, the dominating viewpoint put forth from an individualistic philosophy has now changed our modern morality that skews our research. Shame has become harmful because community has been lost. Not all is lost though, because these researchers have embraced the use of guilt, finding the positive attributes through it, such as repentance and restoration coming from a place of brokenness, as replacing what shame once did.

To drive home this point on the use of shame in our modern world, Brown leaves us with some questions. These questions came out of a story about a judgement in the case of a man battering his wife. The judge forced the man to stand on the steps of City Hall and provide an apology for battering his wife to all of the noontime office workers who were there. Brown quotes the judge as saying,

> "Let those who would beat their wives, steal their neighbor's property and abuse children feel the sting of the community's intolerance, hear their names on our lips and pay the price in full view of the public. Shame on them or shame on us."

Quite poignantly, Brown offers these questions for our reflection.

> "Given what we know about shame and how it affects us, are we safer with him when he's in shame or when he is repairing shame? Are we using shame as a punishment because we think it will foster real change in people? Or are we shaming others because it feels good to make people suffer when we are in fear, anger or judgment?"

Brown offers up a description of vulnerability as a solution to these problems. She describes vulnerability as both a scary place but a strengthening and freeing place to be. This type of vulnerability becomes the healthy expression of Experiential Authority. Through our acceptance of our stories of loss and pain, along with the various expressions of the attached emotions to those stories, we can gain a better understanding of who we are and indeed, who we want to be. As we find language to these emotions, we give a place of equality to our emotional capacities, thus becoming more aware of our intrinsic worth and value. This journey is a vulnerable one and is the positive expression of Experiential Authority. We have an experience that is truly ours and we may share that experience from a place of authority, without inviting the Listener to disregard his or her own experiences for ours.

Vulnerability becomes the vehicle in which this experience is shared and even though it may be shared from a place of authority, there is truly nothing about it that is imposing. In fact, this vulnerability helps open up space for the Listener, inviting them to explore their own stories, finding their own language. Vulnerability, expressed by the Speaker, not only opens up space for the Listener, but also creates a safe place in which the Listener and the Speaker can collaborate. In this context, the Positional Authority that the Speaker has, does not bring the negative aspects of Experiential Authority but instead, through vulnerability, expresses the positive attributes. It is positive because the Speaker recognizes the intrinsic worth and value of the Listener, and from that not-knowing stance, brought forward with the use of vulnerability, the Listener's own experiences are given space in which to be shared in intimate community.

Chapter Eleven External Identities

The idea of an External Identity presses upon the Listener with a roughness and a powerlessness on their part, unable to fight back. Something external from the Listener is being forced upon them, wearing the Listener down under the heavy load of this External Identity. It comes with a sense of confusion and a feeling of being overwhelmed in the Listener's attempt to fight against it. After time, the fight drains from the Listener as they deny who they are or want to be, which is both the objective and result of embracing this new identity.

The Listener feels gross and yucky, but the space to express those emotions is now gone, so the Listener quietly supresses the emotions until the Listener does not hear them any longer. A general sense of unworthiness and a devaluing of self follows this disconnect from the Listener's own emotional experience. The Listener tries to console themselves through a variety of means, as they now work on taking the imposed experiences presented to them from the Speaker and make them theirs. The External Identity imposed upon the Listener has now become their identity; it has become who they are.

Imagine a little girl wearing an over-sized jacket that wraps around her body completely. All you see is a bit of her face as she peers out at a full-length mirror in front of her. The jacket is a thick furry winter jacket and somewhere in the background, you hear an adult's voice saying, "You're a little bear!" This description could easily be for a childhood game, played by the child who would find their parent's clothes and put them on. In the child's innocence, they enter the world of imagination, pretending to be princesses or great heroes. When the parent comes by and offers up the bear description the little girl then looks into the mirror and pretends to be that bear.

What if the Speaker was getting the Listener to put something on and as the Listener looked into the mirror they heard the Speaker's description of what they thought the Listener was - coming from somewhere behind them? Along with this 'jacket' came the mocking voice in the background calling the Listener a bad mother, a loser father, or some other negative description. In the same way that little girl tried on the jacket and became a little bear in the mirror is the same way that the Speaker imposes their identity upon the Listener. The Listener is now standing in front of that mirror looking at how the Speaker has dressed them up, or in other words described who the Listener is.

Often these External Identities form multiple layers upon the Listener. We can now imagine the little girl standing in front of this full-length mirror with multiple layers of jackets on. One by one, another 'jacket' is placed on her, all the while burying the little girl underneath. The little girl can feel the weight of these jackets yet feels powerless to remove any of them. She is then faced with the burden of responding to each of these External Identities and somewhere through this process; she loses touch with who she is and who she wants to be. Now, instead of one voice in the background, there are many and the confusion only adds to the hopelessness of the situation. The little girl has conditioned herself to respond appropriately to each voice, but with her sense of worth and value being connected to each of these External Identities, there is no lasting sense of connectedness. This then leads her to a common place of depression.

This External Identity can be a powerful influencer in our lives, forming these identities from early ages. This is the beginning of Historical Relational Authority. The External Identity began as the result of Experiential Authority, where the Listener was limited in their choices because the Speaker closed down the space to explore the Listener's experience. Consequently, the Listener took on the External Identity being offered by the Speaker who was in a place of Positional Authority in their life. However, as time goes on and this Speaker continues to come in and out of their life, and that continuous reminder and reinforcement of the External Identity is Historical Relational Authority. The result of such an interaction is that the Listener feels compelled to be that person the Speaker is describing from the past. As the Listener tries to resist that contextual description of self, the Listener meets strong resistance from the

Speaker they are trying to interact with.

These imposing descriptions can and do come from significant people in the Listener's lives and over time these significant people tend to reinforce those descriptions of identity upon them. The result is that the Listener will take on these External Identities and try them out – perhaps a reflection of their desire to be wanted, needed, loved, heard, desired, or connected. Whatever the reason for trying out these External Identities, the entire experience leaves the Listener quite badly wounded, or simply feeling quite gross inside. Like the little girl in the mirror, the Listener is now encouraged to walk around and pretend they are that little bear when perhaps all along they wanted to be a princess, or prince, or something else entirely.

External Identities can be difficult to recognize at first because we tend to have several learned behaviours operating in our lives. Learned behaviours are those behaviours that we learn within intimate, closed systems such as families, close friends, or groups such as church communities. Learned behaviours are the varying styles of relating and the various roles that we are expected to perform if we want acceptance and inclusion into these intimate and somewhat closed systems. For the most part, most of us may find ourselves having come from one of these closed systems, like a child in a family. Over time, the child would have learned various roles in order to relate to the ones with power and control within that system. Learned behaviors exist in most every system we are a part of, however in these intimate and closed systems these behaviors are rewarded and reinforced the strongest.

The Listener may first become aware of an External Identity in their lives as a result of a recent conversation with the Speaker. At first the Listener may generally be aware of a yucky feeling they have inside, accentuated from that recent interaction with the Speaker. Using Historical Relational Authority, the Speaker may have once again reminded the Listener of who they should be according to the External Identity that the Speaker assigned to the Listener at some point in the past. Perhaps the only clue to something being wrong with this picture is the Listener's own irritability and a general sense of a lack of worth or a lack of value. The Listener may not make the connection, nor clearly identify what is happening for them, but the emotional language being formed is clear; the Listener feel worthless and devalued and they have no idea why.

The Listener may not be able to identify the source of this worthlessness and yucky-ness as having come out of the conversation with the Speaker. However, in their effort to process their emotional experiences their self-talk may reveal the presence of an External Identity in their life. The Listener may not even be aware that they took on an External Identity but as they seek space in which to explore language for their emotional experience, the

Listener is confronted with these external voices in their head, restricting the space that the Listener is trying to create for themselves. The External Identity continues to press in, until the Listener gives in and accepts the identity and makes it their own.

My advice for this Listener is to pause for a moment and finding a mirror. I would ask them to go and stand in front of it. I would then ask the Listener whom do they see? What jackets is the Listener wearing that has been imposed by others and is in fact hiding who the Listener really is? The biggest step forward in finding a sense of worth and value once again in the Listener's life is to stare long and hard at that mirror, beginning to see those jackets. Next, it is to watch their self as the Listener systematically takes each jacket off.

Slowly, the Listener will let the External Identity fall to the ground as they continue to stare into the mirror. Slowly, the Listener will begin to see the person they want to be and in fact who they have always been. The process of removing these jackets recognizes that they are External Identities all along and do not reflect who the Listener is or more importantly who they want to be. This is how the Listener identifies Experiential Authority. The Listener first finds their own language to describe that yucky-ness and through the act of identifying the Experiential Authority, the Listener ends up stripping it of its authority over them.

When describing these ideas to both clients and individuals I have asked them to pay attention to the messages and voices that they would hear in the background as they are looking in the mirror. By drawing the person's attention to these voices they are better equipped to clearly identify those 'jackets' they have been wearing and consequently feel more empowered to remove them. Differentiating from the external voices of identity and their own voice trying to be heard is the goal of this exercise of looking in the mirror.

In some cases, as the person looked at the mirror they have identified the voices as being quite overwhelming. In an attempt to gain back control from all of these External Identities, I have suggested a strong visual cue in order to shatter the voices and free them from these many jackets. I have suggested that the person or client smash the very mirror that they are looking into. In that moment, the power of those External Identities can be shattered as well. It is violent, harsh, and immediate, but the effects have been powerful and freeing for those who have done it.

In the case of Historical Relational Authority, a loss emerges when the Listener recognizes that the Speaker cannot, or chooses not to relate to who the Listener has become. Instead, the Listener is related to as being someone the Speaker thinks of through his or her own terms at some point in the past. Like my grad reunion, I cannot change what or even how my old classmates relate to who I have now become until they realize that I am no longer who they once thought I was. This sense of loss, experienced by the Listener, invites him or her to a place of vulnerability. In this place, the Listener can take the time to reflect on this loss and pain, instead of seeking out those external experiences that have promises of no pain.

It is a loss, and sometimes a profound one, when the Listener has no choice but to walk away from a relationship because the Speaker cannot or does not want to relate to the person they are now. It is a dangerous and slippery slope if the Listener was to entertain the idea of modifying who they are in order to take on even a bit of the External Identity for the sake of the Speaker and the broken relationship that exists. Even if the Listener wishes they could continue a relationship with the Speaker, nothing healthy can come from taking on that External Identity. In the end, the Speaker will need the Listener to be someone the Listener is not. The Listener needs to focus on being who they are and have become. The two are incompatible.

The exploration of that loss, and its associated language, gives voice to the Listener's emotions and equalizes their emotional capacity with their cognitive capacity. However, the exploration of that loss invites vulnerability on the Listener's part and can be a difficult place to be. During this exploration of the Listener's own stories of loss and pain, they are susceptible to seek out the Speaker's experiences, which seem to come without any pain and loss. If the Listener takes on another Speaker's experience during their own exploration around pain and loss, all the Listener has accomplished is to perpetuate the cycle of harm that they had found themselves trapped in.

My Master's degree in Marriage and Family Counseling had a practicum component, which was a requirement of graduation from the program. During this part of my academic journey, I had been giving a lot of thought to the impact of emotional pain. It had seemed that this was quite a theme in my life, and it had come up again with my class work. In particular, I had just finished one more week of practicum, which is a hands-on counselling environment with our fellow classmates. In the practicum we counsel each other, be counselled ourselves, and then we review the video and analyze our skill, our methods, our intents, and our purposes. Vulnerability is just the beginning requirement of that experience.

Through the practicum, I became aware of my own pain, personal disappointments, and past events in which I was impacted in a negative way. I also became aware that there had been a growing desire to look at those times to discover some strength about myself along with some positive themes that I suspected to have always been present. My desire to do this was because I had always viewed my life through a negative lens, both with what happened to me and how I viewed myself as a participant in those circumstances. The more I was learning about

Narrative Therapy, as a central tenant to my Master's program, the more I became curious about ideas of identity, this idea of whom I have always been.

I was seeing a counselor for a period while working on my degree simply as a way to care for myself with the various aspects of loss and past trauma that inevitably surfaced through the classwork and assignments. I was enjoying who I was in the now and where I was at, but this clashed with the description of the person I thought I was from my past. As I explored these various stories of loss from my past, I was beginning to see what Narrative Therapists call 'Unique Outcomes'. These positive attributes of self were popping up in my stories from my past and although subtle at first it was enough to have me think about whom I really was, even back then. I became focused on exploring more of my story of loss in an effort to discover these silent indicators, which would reveal aspects of my personality that I truly enjoyed in the present, but had thought were never present in my past. This process is a vulnerable one and quite often misunderstood.

This is most apparent if you sit with someone who has absolutely no idea of the descriptions of self you are speaking about. Thus, the skill of sitting in a not-knowing stance comes in, and it became obvious that most of my classmates, myself included, had no real concept of what that looked like. During my time in practicum, the not-knowing challenge for my client and me was justice. My client would present a very opinionated point-of-view on a topic. It was presented, like most point-of-views, as being the correct one, the only right one, and sadness at those who just did not know any better. During our first hour of conversation, I felt this need within me to defend those massive groups of people in society that would have been as easily offended by my client's remarks as I was.

This defensive stance that I took, however, proved to be a detriment in my conversation with my client and we needed to talk about that in our second hour together. The skill for me was to learn to sit with my client without ever feeling the need to defend these point-of-views. I needed to be comfortable with my own position and presuppositions on such matters in order to be present for the client. As it was, these point-of-views, although important to the issue being discussed, was not what the client wanted to discuss. In other words, the client did not come to the conversation saying, "Please help me change my point-of-views on this range of topics".

When I took the turn as the client, it was my experience that my counselor, a different student, had a fascination with the unknown. Specifically the counselor was drawn to my stories of my dissociation. This fascination grew to the point that instead of focusing on what I said, their focus was on what I did. Because of my spiritual background and dissociative behaviors, I had a heightened sense of my environment at all times. As a way of keeping myself safe, I have a particular way of operating and analyzing my environment that had seemed to have grown to a full out curiosity with my counselor. Specifically, there was a need to understand this uniqueness about me. They were not able to remain in a place of not-knowing as their need to know and understand got the best of them. I could appreciate this, and I could understand the importance of understanding, but my counsellor ended up not handling that knowledge very well.

I felt I was in a circus sideshow or invited to a party to show off my party tricks. There was no hearing or analyzing of what I said but only in what I did. My counsellor highlighted this all the more painfully through their actions. In my counsellor's presentations to our class, to my peers, and to my professors, it felt like there was this ignorant and shameful exposing of this 'trick'. I felt like George from the television series "Seinfeld", shouting out, "I was in the pool! I was in the pool! It was cold!" Standing their naked and deprived of my maleness, my identity, redefined through the eyes of my classmates who seemed focused on the trick over the person. As a result, I shut down emotionally in an effort to survive the experience.

The very issue that I brought to my counsellor compounded this negative experience. I wanted to examine that 'other story' in my life, that story of freedom, and that story who defines Michael in all his wholeness and completeness. In my desire to be present and participatory in every situation, I needed to expose my vulnerability and my fear to my counsellor, in hopes that I could find the freedom there to be so. Instead I found a cage in which I was stuffed into and paraded out in front of the crowds. The lesson learnt from this is the need for a counsellor to sit with the client in a place of not-knowing. This is where the damage occurred with me. My counsellor did not know and was hell-bent on knowing.

Knowing came at a price and that price was caring. The counselor felt that they needed to understand in order to 'help' me. However, in their knowledge seeking, my counselor became captivated with what they discovered. However, because my counselor did not yet fully know, they exposed that lack of knowledge to their peers. If I am going to be truly effective in sitting with a client, I need to be content to allow their point-of-view to flourish in the conversation without any need to administer justice from where I sit, and I need to be able to sit with them in a not-knowing stance without any need to know. I need to allow the client to guide me, lead me, and I will follow, forever curious, and always seeking and exploring with them. Anything else can destroy and harm the client more than they already have been. Lesson learnt. Painfully learnt. Painfully experienced. Hopefully painfully freeing.

The Listener seeks affirmation in community and desires a connectedness. Out of that place, safety is established, and given healthy boundaries, the Listener can then explore their own vulnerability, finding voice and language to their own emotional experiences. This is an important part of equalizing one's emotional capacities with their cognitive capacities. It is also a prerequisite toward understanding who one is, apart from the various External Identities that they have interacted with throughout their lifetimes. Woven into these safe and intimate communities are complex relationships, where intimacy is created and sustained. Within the structure of these relationships is an equal distribution of power, freely given and shared in the back and forth flow of these various relationships. Over time, these relationships change as we do, adjusting to our new realities of self and circumstance.

Death is the great equalizer of power. It violently rips any perception of power we had from our hands and leaves us standing there in our barren states for all to see. The rules changed with death, and no longer do any boundaries or issues of authoritative power exist. In one final gesture, the scales were topped up, power redistributed, and in the grief of the loved ones left behind, power is equalized for a moment. I find it interesting that given the idea that power is always at work in every relationship, and a normal expression of power is the mutually giving and taking of that power, that in death it would initially seem like the one who died has taken all the power from the living. However, such an idea is absurd, and we can rationally dismiss the idea that in death one final lunge at holding power was never existent in the first place.

Power seems to be an entity that exists outside of the person. Narrative Therapy uses a technique called the Externalization of the Problem, which means that the person is not the problem but that the problem is the problem. By externalizing the problem, the person can begin to identify with the problem as being separate from them, and therefore find a new way to talk about and explore the problem, working in collaboration to minimize the impact of the problem in their lives. I believe that this may be a helpful way to think about the role of power in a relationship. It is interesting to observe the perception of power in a relationship where you can ask each person in a conflicted relationship, who holds the power? More than likely, both will indicate that the other does. If we were to help this couple externalize power from their relationship, it may help them begin to work collaboratively on minimizing the role of power in their relationship.

We are never free of problems, and there will always be conflicts that exist in relationships, however the impacts of those conflicts are minimized when the couple learns to communicate and work collaboratively on solving the problem. Such is my idea about power. Power exists in every relationship and will always exist, but what would power look like if a couple who has successfully externalized power begin to work collaboratively on minimizing the role of power in their relationship. May I suggest that such a collaborative conversation can begin to create the space for the couple to explore language for their emotional experiences and to build safety for one another in order to have those conversations?

Death, then, is the reminder to each of us that power is an illusion, albeit a powerful illusion. It leaves the living standing there with nothing in their hands, and reminds them that there was nothing there to begin with. Thus, in that moment of loss, one is reminded that the struggle for power was in vain, which only serves to accentuate the loss in the present. This idea of illusionary power should prompt us to re-examine the role that power is playing in our current relationships, and then be spurred on to work collaboratively in order to externalize the role of power. In this process, power's authority is removed and the coldness of death's reminder has not gone in vain.

This presence of power in a relationship is helpful in the sense that it leads us to a greater understanding of ourselves, of who we are, and who we want to be. In particular, this understanding is played out in the various relationships we have as a part of our lives. Power and its use help define that identity and when used in healthy ways, it affirms that identity, always drawing out the best in us. A lot of our early development around ideas of identity comes out of the family system that we were a part of, which comprises an intimate community. This early family system then does it part to affirm us in both a personal identity and a cultural identity.

For the most part, if we can assume that our early development happened in relatively healthy family systems, we would enter adolescence with a healthy sense of who we are. However, given typical developmental patterns our entrance into adolescence tends to challenge our sense of identity. "Who am I?" is the often silent screamed question of a teenager, and given the void in which the question is poised, the question often follows the teenager into early adulthood. If trauma or loss are combined with such a norm, then I speculate that the question is silenced, and the person learns to fit nice and neatly into the societal box being imposed upon them. Eventually, however, the box no longer fits with the seams bursting apart to reveal someone who does not know who they are.

As the person begins to explore this long buried question of who they are, they may begin to discover that who they are is in fact who they have always been, outside of the box in which society has stuffed them, that is. The analogy of a monarch butterfly is a helpful illustration to explain what I am referring to here. A caterpillar begins its life as a caterpillar and eventually it goes through metamorphosis and emerges a butterfly. However, the butterfly was always a butterfly, even when it was a caterpillar, and especially when it was tightly bound in its cocoon. To carry this analogy just one-step further, the emergence of the butterfly from the cocoon is both a beautiful process and a violent one. There exists this idea that no matter what, when a person decides for themselves who they are, that is both a violent and beautiful thing to see.

The violence is associated with the box bursting, the breaking away from imposing descriptions of self from others, the labeling and the mocking when a person 'tries something new'. The beauty is in the affirmation of self that comes when a person stretches out into this new description, not one imposed, but one carefully crafted by self, and affirmed in the intimacy of community. Simply put, I do not want anyone to tell me who I am or worse who I ought to be. As I desire to seek power equality in all of my relationships, it is first important for me to be comfortable with whom I am. From that place of self-description, I can lovingly offer self to those around me, and joyfully invite them into relationship with me, without needing them to define me, or see me in some imposed box from long ago.

I can be transparent with them, I can be vulnerable with them, I can be honest with them, and most importantly, I can be me with them. Out of that environment, I will find intimate affirmation of self, and in that environment, there is no longer an unbalancing of power or authority. Although these cultural boxes that we burst forth from play a big part in the formation of who we are, I am not interested in having my description of self be limited to any box. In the same way, the butterfly should not be limited to the description of the cocoon or even the previous form of a caterpillar. We should now have the freedom to experience self, and to become comfortable with who we are and who we want to be. This, then, becomes our identity, the culmination of our experiences.

Our experiences direct truths for us far more then we really give them credit for. The acceptance of something as being 'correct' or 'truth', especially when compared to something else of similar form being 'wrong', is only defined as such by the user. This comes through in all situations requiring comparison, or when issues or arguments are weighed against each other. I find it fascinating to watch people do this regularly. Out of their own personal experience, whether they are truly aware of it or not, they will redefine what is right and what is wrong. My children did this; years ago after having a Chinese meal, only to have the effects of the flu descend upon them that same evening. Now, years later, only one of my children have decided to give Chinese food a second chance, and loving it too.

My observation goes beyond Chinese food, however, and into those types of experiences that carry power and authority with them. I chuckle to myself whenever I know of a female friend who is pregnant as I enjoy asking the question, "So, how many women have approached you today with reams of 'advice' about your pregnancy?" This becomes even more amusing when I find out that some of those women have never been pregnant. However, it is not all chuckles though, because harm can occur in these situations as well. Religion is a hard topic for these types of conversations as is politics, and social commentary. Even this book comes from a place of reflective observation of relational dynamics, based out of my understanding of relational dynamics, but limited to my contextual setting.

My limited scope - the bubble in which I live - has helped define what is 'right' and what is 'truth'. I therefore share these observations with power and authority with you, inviting collaborative conversations about them. Nonetheless, I must be aware that the scope of what I present here is limited to what I have studied, observed, and experienced all within a contextual setting. This is where curiosity comes in. It seems to me that curiosity can take on the role of a helpful corrective in conversation. It holds back our tongues, slows down our minds, and helps us remain more attentive to our co-conversationalist. Curiosity reminds us - or should remind us - that we have not necessarily found what is 'right' or 'truth' but have only come to 'experience' something as being 'right' and 'true'. It is in these curious conversations that we are stretched and challenged to think more about our experiences related to our convictions.

So we can listen, we can be aware of our own presuppositions, and we can be vulnerable all in an effort to avoid the harmful effects of Experiential Authority. However, without first understanding our own intrinsic worth and value we may be susceptible to the Speaker's External

Identity being imposed upon us. This would include the Speaker's own definitions of worth and value woven throughout that External Identity. In combating the harmful effects of Experiential Authority, we must learn to say no. Saying no becomes that definitive action against Experiential Authority. We may say it verbally or internally, and in either case the action associated with no creates space for us to think our own thoughts, resist those imposing descriptions from the Speaker, and to help us find our own language to our emotional experience.

Saying no to Experiential Authority also means saying yes to our experiences of loss and pain, and being okay with listening to our own journeys through those stories. These journeys have contributed to who we are and so we should work to minimize the effects of Experiential Authority on them. Take both the time and the space to understand and appreciate the intrinsic worth and value that each of us have as a place to begin. Take the time to listen to our emotions as they have very important things to say. Be aware of our own presuppositions in conversations with others along with the various dynamics associated with relational power. All of these elements will help minimize Experiential Authority in our lives and keep us from using Experiential Authority on others.

I have introduced the language of Experiential Authority here as a way of explaining the yucky and gross feeling that we get sometimes after leaving a conversation. In my explanation, I began with unpacking my own presuppositions and personal journey, which has helped shape the various ideas around Experiential Authority. This is language I offer tentatively to you, my reader, in hopes that you may find it helpful, as you explore your own journey. I hold the language out tentatively for you to look at and interact with. I hope you find it helpful in minimizing the harm of others in your life.

About The Author

 Michael Towers was born in Enderby, British Columbia. Over the last forty years, Michael has moved over thirty times. In 2008, Michael, his wife, and their six children, changed directions, moving to Saskatchewan so Michael could finish his Master's degree in Marriage and Family Counseling. He currently is working as a Director for an inner-city mission located in Regina, Saskatchewan. This is his first book, which was a result of his research during his Master's degree.

Manufactured by Amazon.ca
Bolton, ON

40821144R00125